New and Selected Poems

1974–2004

Also by Carl Dennis

Carl Dennis

New and Selected Poems

1974–2004

PENGUIN POETS

PENGUIN BOOKS

Published by the Penguin Group
Penguin Group (USA) Inc., 375 Hudson Street,
New York, New York 10014, U.S.A.
Penguin Books Ltd, 80 Strand,
London WC2R 0RL, England
Penguin Books Australia Ltd, 250 Camberwell Road, Camberwell,
Victoria 3124, Australia
Penguin Books Canada Ltd, 10 Alcorn Avenue,
Toronto, Ontario, Canada M4V 3B2
Penguin Books India (P) Ltd, 11 Community Centre, Panchsheel Park,
New Delhi – 110 017, India
Penguin Books (N.Z.) Ltd, Cnr Rosedale and Airborne Roads, Albany,
Auckland, New Zealand
Penguin Books (South Africa) (Pty) Ltd, 24 Sturdee Avenue,
Rosebank, Johannesburg 2196, South Africa

Penguin Books Ltd, Registered Offices:
80 Strand, London WC2R 0RL, England

First published in Penguin Books 2004

1   3   5   7   9   10   8   6   4   2

Copyright © Carl Dennis, 2004
All rights reserved

The selections from *Ranking the Wishes* and *Practical Gods* are reprinted by permission
of Penguin Books, a division of Penguin Group (USA) Inc.

Pages vii and viii constitute an extension of this copyright page.

LIBRARY OF CONGRESS CATALOGING IN PUBLICATION DATA
Dennis, Carl, 1939–   .
[Poems. Selections]
New and selected poems, 1974–2004 / Carl Dennis.
p.   cm.
ISBN 0-14-200083-3
I. Title.
PS3554.E535N48 2004
811'.54—dc22   2003060720

Printed in the United States of America
Set in Garamond 3
Designed by Sabrina Bowers

For Thomas Centolella,

Mark Halliday, and

Tony Hoagland

Acknowledgments

Thanks are due to the editors of the following magazines, in which poems that were later published in book form first appeared:

From NEW POEMS—*American Scholar* ("Socrates and I"), *Atlanta Review* ("Sensible Summers"), *Hunger Mountain* ("The Actor"), *The Paris Review* ("Our Death" and "Window Boxes"), *Parnassus* ("Dream Theory"), *Poetry* ("Candles," "A Colleague Confesses," "Delphinium," "In Paris," "The Master of Metaphor," "The Next Life," and "World History"), *Poetry International* ("Verona"), *Salmagundi* ("Gravestones," "In the Coffee Shop," and "Manners"), and *Smartish Pace* ("From a Practical Reader")

From A HOUSE OF MY OWN, ©1974 by Carl Dennis, originally published by George Braziller—*Concerning Poetry* ("Useful Advice"), *Ktaadn* ("Students"), *Modern Poetry Studies* ("Knots"), and *The New Yorker* ("Relatives")

From CLIMBING DOWN, ©1976 by Carl Dennis, originally published by George Braziller—*Crazy Horse* ("The Peaceable Kingdom") and *Poetry Northwest* ("Native Son")

From SIGNS AND WONDERS, ©1979 by Carl Dennis, originally published by Princeton University Press—*Concerning Poetry* ("Carpentry"), *Laurel Review* ("Near Idaville"), *The New Yorker* ("Snow"), *Salmagundi* ("Grandmother and I"), *South Dakota Review* ("The Tree"), and *Virginia Quarterly Review* ("The Band")

From THE NEAR WORLD, ©1985 by Carl Dennis, originally published by William Morrow and Company—*American Poetry Review* ("Charity"), *Kenyon Review* ("What Has Become of Them"), *The New Republic* ("Hector's Return" and "Later"), *The New Yorker* ("The Midlands" and "More Music"), and *Salmagundi* ("At Home with Cézanne," "Beauty Exposed," and "Captain Cook")

From THE OUTSKIRTS OF TROY, ©1988 by Carl Dennis, originally published by William Morrow and Company—*Ironwood* ("At Becky's Piano Recital"), *The New Yorker* ("On the Soul"), *Poetry* ("Fear of the Dark," "Heinrich Schliemann," and "On the Way to School"), *Salmagundi* ("Henry James and Hester Street" and "The Promised Land"), and *Sonora Review* (Part III of "Twenty Years")

From MEETINGS WITH TIME, ©1992 by Carl Dennis, originally published by Viking Penguin—*Agni* ("Infidels"), *American Poetry Review* ("Unfinished Symphony"), *Denver Quarterly* ("Adventure," "The Bill of Rights," and "Haven"), *Kenyon Review* ("Tuesday at First Presbyterian"), *Poetry* ("Defining Time," "No Shame," "Spring Letter," and "The Window"), *Prairie Schooner* ("Night Walk" and "The Photograph"), *Salmagundi* ("The Anthropic Cosmological Principle"), *Shenandoah* ("The Window in the Spring"), and *Virginia Quarterly Review* ("My Guardians")

From RANKING THE WISHES, ©1997 by Carl Dennis, published by Penguin Books—*Agni* ("All I've Wanted"), *American Poetry Review* ("Days of Heaven," "Pendulum," and "Sarit Narai"), *Atlantic Monthly* ("Bivouac Near Trenton"), *Kenyon Review* ("Seven Days" and "Two or Three Wishes"), *The New Republic* ("Consolation" and "Grace"), *The Paris Review* ("The Great Day" and "Integer"), *Ploughshares* ("Distinctions" and "Writing at Night"), *Poetry* ("As If," "Loss," "Still Life," and "To Reason"), and *Virginia Quarterly Review* ("Starry Night" and "Your City")

From PRACTICAL GODS, ©2001 by Carl Dennis, published by Penguin Books—*American Poetry Monthly* ("More Art"), *American Poetry Review* ("Audience"), *American Scholar* ("Eurydice"), *The Nation* ("To a Pagan"), *The New Republic* ("Bashō," "Bishop Berkeley," "History," and "On the Bus to Utica"), *Pivot* ("*Gelati*"), *Poetry* ("Eternal Life," "Eternal Poetry," "Jesus Freaks," "Not the Idle," "Progressive Health," "Prophet," "Saint Francis and the Nun," "School Days," and "Sunrise"), *Prairie Schooner* ("The Serpent to Adam"), *Salmagundi* ("The God Who Loves You," "The Lace Maker," "A Letter from Mary in the Tyrol," and "View of Delft"), and *Tri-Quarterly* ("May Jen")

I also want to thank the generous friends who gave me valuable criticism on many of these poems: Charles Altieri, Thomas Centolella, Alan Feldman, Mark Halliday, Tony Hoagland, and Martin Pops.

Contents

New Poems

Gravestones	3
Heroic	5
Socrates and I	7
Manners	9
Verona	11
A Colleague Confesses	14
In Paris	16
Delphinium	18
In the Coffee Shop	20
Window Boxes	22
The Next Life	24
Our Death	26
From a Practical Reader	27
The Master of Metaphor	29
Sensible Summers	30
Manifesto	32
World History	34
The Actor	36
Dream Theory	37
Candles	39

from
A House of My Own (1974)

Useful Advice	43
Students	44
Relatives	45
Knots	46

from
Climbing Down (1976)

Ingratitude	49
The Homeowner	50
The Peaceable Kingdom	51
Praise for My Heart	52
Native Son	53

from
Signs and Wonders (1979)

Listeners	57
Near Idaville	58
Carpentry	60
Snow	61
The Tree	62
Sunday	63
Grandmother and I	64
A Plea for More Time	66
The Band	67

from
The Near World (1985)

Hector's Return	71
At the Corner	73
The Midlands	75
Beauty Exposed	76
Captain Cook	78
At Home with Cézanne	80

More Music   82
What Has Become of Them   83
Later   84
Charity   86
Time Heals All Wounds   87

from
The Outskirts of Troy (1988)

Heinrich Schliemann   91
The Promised Land   92
Henry James and Hester Street   93
Visiting a Friend Near Sagamon Hill   95
Twenty Years   97
Little League   103
Fear of the Dark   104
On the Soul   105
At Becky's Piano Recital   106
The Circus   108
On the Way to School   110

from
Meetings with Time (1992)

The Photograph   115
Defining Time   117
My Guardians   119
Tuesday at First Presbyterian   120
The Window in Spring   122
Haven   124
Adventure   126

The Bill of Rights 129
The Invalid 131
The Anthropic Cosmological Principle 133
Unfinished Symphony 135
Mildew 137
Night Walk 139
Infidel 141
My Moses 143
Delaware Park, 1990 144
Spring Letter 146
Invitation 148
No Shame 150

from
Ranking the Wishes (1997)

Loss 155
Pendulum 157
Days of Heaven 159
To Reason 161
Cedar Point 163
The Great Day 165
Seven Days 167
Sarit Narai 168
Aunt Celia, 1961 171
All I've Wanted 173
Integer 175
Distinctions 176
Two or Three Wishes 178
Grace 179
Bivouac Near Trenton 181

Consolation   182
Writing at Night   184
As If   186
Starry Night   188
Still Life   189
Your City   190

from
Practical Gods (2001)

A Priest of Hermes   195
Saint Francis and the Nun   196
Department Store   198
Not the Idle   200
Gelati   201
To a Pagan   203
History   204
School Days   206
Prophet   210
Pride   212
On the Bus to Utica   213
Jesus Freaks   215
The Serpent to Adam   217
View of Delft   218
A Chance for the Soul   220
Audience   222
A Letter from Mary in the Tyrol   224
Numbers   226
The Fallen   228
Eurydice   230
The Lace Maker   231

Progressive Health   233
More Art   235
Bashō   237
Improbable Story   239
Bishop Berkeley   241
Sunrise   243
Eternal Poetry   245
In the Short Term   247
Guardian Angel   249
May Jen   251
Eternal Life   252
The God Who Loves You   254

New Poems

Gravestones

It's easy to mock sarcophagi for their wish to impress us,
But not the modest tablets with their brief inscriptions:
"Beloved wife," "beloved husband," parent or child
Or friend. One stone in Buffalo's Forest Lawn,
Just a few steps from the grave of Millard Fillmore,

Says only, "Not here, not here,"
Under a woman's name, no birth or death date.
Not here if you seek her spirit, seems the simplest reading,
Her spirit having ascended to its real home.
Or else the doubling of the phrase alters the mood

From assertive finality to wish, to prayer:
May her essence be active elsewhere still,
Not buried here. It's either that or a cry of loss:
Wherever she is, she isn't here anymore
Alive and well, casting a light around her

To restore our spirits. As for the stones too worn
To be read, their silence advises the passersby
To put away the longing to be remembered
And concentrate on the wish to lie
Calm on their deathbeds, friends and family

Pressing in close for a final blessing.
Whoever can't witness the end, or won't,
May visit the grave to transact some private business.
Now that you're far away, I can forgive you.
Or now that you're quiet you can forgive me.

Only a portion of me was turned against you.
The better portion stood in the wings beside the other,

And was just as ready to make an entrance
When the cue came and give a speech as heartfelt
As the bitter words that elbowed their way on stage.

Listen. You can sleep later. Until you help,
Sleep will never visit you anyway
If you're still the person you used to be
And understand how much you're needed,
How a sign from you can set me free.

Heroic

"There is no comfort in life away from people
Who care for you," writes Minny Temple,
In 1869, from Newport, where she's resting
After the third episode, in three days,
Of coughing blood. "Not a heroic statement,"
She adds, "I'm fully aware."

At the age of twenty-three, "heroic" for her
Means lofty and lonely, a lone commitment
She supposes herself too needy to carry through.
Still, her passion for life as death approaches
Now seems heroic enough, her concern
With feeling deeply and thinking rightly.

"Don't be afraid of hurting my feelings,"
She writes to her cousin Henry, who's mentioned
How different he thinks they are, but withheld particulars,
"Though there's no one," she adds, "whose sympathy
Would encourage me so much as yours."
She's prepared to listen humbly "to the worst"

If it helps improve her fidelity to her "deepest instincts."
Her belief that such fidelity is a high vocation
Not to be abandoned as her body abandons her
Inspired her cousin, thirty years later,
To provide a woman like her with a plot and setting
Fit for the heroine of a tragedy.

Though Minny wouldn't have wanted to die in Venice
Away from her family, like James's protagonist,
In a palace that suits a princess, she did want to see Europe
Before the end. Too bad no one she cared to go with

Was able to take her, or willing, though her doctor
Opined that a warmer climate would do her good.

It seems heroic of her not to have asked her cousin
And not to have blamed him for never offering.
Heroic to believe "dear Harry" a hero
For steaming off by himself toward the independence
His writing required, a mistress more demanding
Than any invalid friend, more jealous.

If he didn't regret his choice, he still may have felt his spirit
Smaller than hers. The spirit he gives his heroine
Is large enough to forgive her friends their inconstancy.
Bereft as they leave her feeling, she spreads her wings
With a grace unstinted and unconditional
That the author knew he could not provide.

Socrates and I

Faced with his decision after the assembly
Votes against him and he's led back to his cell,
I'd have listened to his friends' escape plan.
Still I'm glad he refuses, glad that for him
Breaking the laws of Athens,
Even when they're applied unjustly,
Would be like breaking the hearts of parents
Who've never been false to their obligations.

It does me good to see him defining self-interest
As something larger than self-protection.
It makes me want to believe that if my Athens
Here in western New York, on the Niagara,
Had him arrested as a public menace,
He wouldn't promise our Common Council
That if they released him without a trial
He'd talk from then on only with friends,
In private, as I might promise.

It's bracing to meet a man who's certain
There's only one life for him, questioning everyone.
As for the afterlife, he imagines asking the dead
Just what he's asked the living—what's justice, what's piety,
Who's wise, who only seems so—though in Hades
He could talk without fear of interruption.

In that regard Buffalo's an improvement too.
I can't blame anyone but myself if I find no time
To turn my talk to the big questions.
No dinner of mine will be spoiled by news
That Rochester's joined with Erie in a pincer maneuver
And will soon be upon us. Our fleet is safe

From the fleet of Syracuse. Our sailors
Will die in their beds, not in the quarries,
After a calm farewell to their families.

As for the last words Socrates says
As the chill of the hemlock rises to his heart—
"I owe a cock to Asclepius"—
I admit they seem less of a bracing insight
Than a conundrum. Why is it right as he dies
To thank the god of healing for a recovery?
Still I'm grateful to him for his refusal
Of any deathbed magniloquence and feel obliged
To take issue with Nietzsche, who reads him as meaning
Life is a sickness, death a release.

"Can't you see," I say, "that he feels blessed
To be able to end his life as he lived it,
Loyal to one luminous purpose?"
And Nietzsche, after pondering for a while,
Is inspired enough by his master's example
Not to grow scornful, aloof, or sullen,
As he points to shadows in my lamp-lit room.

Manners

No notes in this book on the early settling of America
Bought at the airport, so no way of knowing
Which tribe it refers to when it mentions one
That assumed the restless, pale-faced strangers
Had sailed across the sea to learn good manners.
But whatever its name, assuming the statement accurate,
It must have learned its mistake in a month or two.

No facts, only interpretations, as Nietzsche says,
But some interpretations will do us in
While others enable our tribe to continue
Doing what it does best, our priests and prophets
Passing good manners down to the next generation
Like the steps of a dance or the recipe for an elixir.

Thanks for coming so far to join us this evening
For a banquet of fish cakes, walnuts, and cherries.
We're going to take your silence as shy approval.
We're going to take your refusal of second helpings
As a failure in training, not of intentions.
You want to be mannerly but don't know how.

As for any stray look of calculation
That betrays an intention to do us harm,
We believe you're capable of remorse at any moment.
Here is the tent where you'll sleep tonight
Dreaming of your gods' approval as we of ours.
May they rank good manners higher than making converts.
May they feel they've all the worshipers they can handle
And be grateful that other gods are lending a hand.

Here's to the gods who teach good manners
By good example, who never hurt our feelings
By complaining they've had to withdraw their perfection
From a precinct of being to make room for us,
Us creatures far from perfect. Here's to their courtesy
In claiming their bad backs and wobbly knees
Keep them from bending to dust the corners,
So they'd really be grateful for our help.

Verona

I'd have come here decades sooner
If one of my art books had devoted a chapter
To beautiful central squares
And this piazza had been included,
Bright with façades meant to be festive,
Not magnificent or imposing.
Even the two earnest young men in suits
Buttonholing strollers don't dull my pleasure,
Two Mormons from Utah, assigned to this outpost
For their stint as apostles among the gentiles.

A city not on the list that Burton and I
Drew up thirty years ago when we planned
His only chance to see Europe before his eyes
Would grow too scarred from the stress of diabetes
To let the light in. In the end, he felt too gloomy to go.
If he were alive now, and sighted, we'd agree
These two young Mormons have a tough assignment,
Making the gospel revealed to Joseph Smith
Near Palmyra, New York, irresistible
To churchgoing Veronese whose kin
Have sung in the local choirs for centuries.

As for lifting the spirits of nonbelievers,
I've only to pause on a bridge spanning the Adige
And gaze back on the fillet of walls and towers
The river looks pleased to wear.
Even Burton, always harder to please than I,
Might have been moved to judge this townscape
Nearly as peaceful as a townscape in oil,
Though its Sunday quiet, he might have cautioned,

Shouldn't make us forget the weekday broils
Stirred up by the likes of the Montagues and the Capulets.

If the Mormons regard these streets merely as a backdrop
For preaching to passersby, they commit a sin
Against the church of the beautiful that Burton
Tried to visit in his cheerful moods. Streets
As an end in themselves or streets as a starting point
For a painting that offers an ideal landscape,
One of Poussin's, say, that moves the viewer to rise
For at least a moment from a mood that's passing
To a mood more permanent, however uncommon.

If the two apostles suppose the actual landscape
Will surpass Poussin's in tranquillity of the spirit
Once their gospel is acknowledged by everyone,
They join a crowd of prophets whose promises
Made Burton angry. Better not wait around,
He would have told them, for slugs
To change into butterflies. Better work instead
At making the stubbornly untransformed
Care about learning to vote for candidates
Likely to serve the city, though they realize
Their city is only the roughest sketch of Poussin's.

In my favorite painting of his, the city's a distant line
Near the horizon. The human figures set in the foreground
Are thumb-sized blues and yellows in a field of green.
It's harvest time, and among the harvesters
The Capulets and the Montagues are swinging their scythes.
Also the Mormon boys, no longer in summer suits

But garbed like peasants, steadily working beside them
While Pan and Flora look on from a stand of willows.

And Burton is there with his sight restored,
Pointing to a stand of birch where the workers
Can rest in the shade and admire the view.
And here he is later, returning to ask the rested
If they'd help him load more bales on the wagon
For the last trip of the day to the barn.

A Colleague Confesses

Now that we've gotten along as office mates
For three semesters, I don't mind letting you know,
In confidence, that the poems and stories we're teaching
Are less important to me than they are to you.
However beautiful in themselves, they don't uplift me
As meditation uplifted me when I was a disciple.
To be sure, I gave up the discipline after a year,
Unable, finally, to empty my mind enough
For the kind of harmony with the void
Enjoyed by the few enlightened.
Now, in my fallback mode, I try to content myself
With working at harmony with the world.

I want to know what it's like to be other people
And am always practicing, weekdays with students
And colleagues, weekends with strangers.
Even in the car alone, on a Sunday drive,
I move my lips with the preachers on the radio
As I imagine what longing pushes them forward.
As for the satisfied, what right have I to judge them,
To declare they shouldn't be happy
With the raises they've earned or the holiday reservations
They've called in early enough to book the rooms
They covet, facing the ocean?

I wouldn't know what to say if they asked me
Point-blank about the life I believe they're missing.
As for the books we're teaching,
I think I respond to their plots and characters
As fully as anyone, but I have to confess
I don't regard them as throwing much light
On the world beyond the page. True to experience,

Now and then, the best ones, maybe,
But not to something experience merely hints at,
Something more spacious and longer lasting.

It seems odd that the books likely to last
Can only acknowledge that nothing lasts but wishes.
Am I leaving out something that stories and poems
Help you see clearly? Spell it out, if you think so.
I'm not too set in my ways to listen.

In Paris

Today as we walk in Paris I promise to focus
More on the sights before us than on the woman
We noticed yesterday in the photograph at the print shop,
The slender brunette who looked like you
As she posed with a violin case by a horse-drawn omnibus
Near the Luxembourg Gardens. Today I won't linger long
On the obvious point that her name is as lost to history
As the name of the graveyard where her bones
Have been crumbling to dust for over a century.
The streets we're to wander will shine more brightly
Now that it's clear the day of her death
Is of little importance compared to the moment
Caught in the photograph as she makes her way
Through afternoon light like this toward the Seine.
The cold rain that fell this morning has given way to sunshine.
The gleaming puddles reflect our mood
Just as they reflected hers as she stepped around them
Smiling to herself, happy that her audition
An hour before went well. After practicing scales
For years in a village whose name isn't recorded,
She can study in Paris with one of the masters.
No way of telling now how close her life
Came to the life she hoped for as she rambled,
On the day of the photograph, along the quay.
But why do I need to know when she herself,
If offered a chance to peruse the book of the future,
Might shake her head no and turn away?
She wants to focus on her afternoon, now almost gone,
As we want to focus on ours as we stand
Here on the bridge she stood on to watch
The steamers push up against the current or ease down.
This flickering light on the water as the boats pass by

Is the flow that many painters have tried to capture
Without holding too still. By the time these boats arrive
Far off in the provinces and give up their cargoes,
Who knows where the flow may have carried us?
But to think now of our leaving is to wrong the moment.
We have to be wholly here as she was
If we want the city that welcomed her
To welcome us as students trained in her school
To enjoy the music as much as she did
When she didn't grieve that she couldn't stay.

Delphinium

How and why their ancestors slowly moved out
From the home pool of algae scum
Onto dry land to make a meadow
Is hidden now. No dream possessed them,
That much is clear, of founding a new nation
Free of old-world law, old-world opinion.
To say they wanted to be delphinium
Is to force upon them a life within
They have no use for. And if they're blue
Because the competition with other flowers for bees
Happened to be less fierce in that band of the spectrum,
If the shape of their buds reminded the male bee
Of the female, it's anyone's guess why the plant
Grew like a column, not like a bouquet or spray.
It looks like a tower rising above the roofs
For viewing the ships of friends or enemies
Sailing into the bay, though the flowers themselves
Are sightless. Good thing our admiring glances,
Unnoticed by them, can't puff them with pride,
The pride that goeth before a fall. As for the fall
That will soon be upon them, their ignorance
As their one and only future dwindles to zero
Marks a gap between them and us
That can't be closed. Still if sentiment moves you
You're free to regard each sprig as an orphan
And tend some yourself, a foster parent
Nursing a baby through mumps and measles.
It shows a big heart to offer succor
Without the expectation of gratitude, though later
The sight of their blue spires
Upright under a leaden sky may seem like a gift.
None looks disheartened, confused, or querulous.

None attempts to flatter you with the question,
"What am I, a delphinium, that thou,
Great gardener, should be mindful?"

In the Coffee Shop

The big smile the waitress gives you
May be a true expression of her opinion
Or may be her way to atone for glowering
A moment ago at a customer who slurped his coffee
Just the way her cynical second husband slurped his.

Think of the meager tip you left the taxi driver
After the trip from the airport, how it didn't express
Your judgment about his service but about the snow
That left you feeling the earth a tundra
Only the frugal few could hope to cross.

Maybe it's best to look for fairness
Not in any particular unbiased judgment
But in a history of mistakes that balance out,
To find an equivalent for the pooling of tips
Practiced by the staff of the coffee shop,
Adding them up and dividing, the same to each.

As for the chilly fish eye the busboy gave you
When told to clear the window table you wanted,
It may have been less a comment on you
Than on his parents, their dismissing the many favors
He does for them as skimpy installments
On a debt too massive to be paid off.

And what about favors you haven't earned?
The blonde who's passing the window now
Without so much as a glance in your direction
Might be trying to focus her mind on her performance
So you, or someone like you, will be pleased to watch

As she crosses the square in her leather snow boots
And tunic of red velvet, fur-trimmed.

What have you done for her that she should turn
The stones of the public buildings
Into a backdrop, a crosswalk into a stage floor,
A table in a no-frills coffee shop
Into a private box near the orchestra?

Yesterday she may have murmured against the fate
That keeps her stuck in the provinces.
But today she atones with her wish to please
As she dispenses with footlights and spotlights,
With a curtain call at the end, with encores.
No way to thank her but with attention
Now as she nears the steps of the courthouse
And begins her unhurried exit into the crowd.

Window Boxes

Even the few on my street who regard themselves as aliens
Declare with their window boxes that they're not ungrateful
For the happenstance of being alive,
That they're just as responsive to the balmy June air
As old Mrs. Ford on the street of my childhood,
Whose window boxes made everyone pause in wonder.

In her loneliness after her husband died,
She would have left St. Louis, my mother said,
And moved to her daughter's house in Chicago
If it weren't for her brother downtown in the asylum;
And still she deemed her flowers worth the effort.

Asylum, that was the word back then,
As if the residents down on Arsenal Street
Had fled there from persecution, a platoon of Dantes
Come to Ravenna, city of colored mosaics
And gem-like flowers, after Florence disowned them.

Not many flowers at Mrs. Ford's funeral
With only six people attending, her daughter and son-in-law
And four neighbors, my brother and I among them,
To help with the coffin. A shame that her window boxes,
Left to their fate, didn't receive the care
From the new owner that people here
Seem glad to provide, some more than others.

Lilies of the valley, astilbe, and woodruff
Do much in their modest way to brighten

The shady side of the street while begonias
And daisies bask on the sunny.

At the graveside, the minister
Read of the sparrow whose fall is noted by heaven
And numbered in a portfolio that must have grown
At last too heavy to carry. It's hard to blame
The scribe grown old in service for retiring
To a solitude beyond the world
And contenting himself with the few acres
That he can handle, window-box tending
Compared to his former cosmic husbandry.

How festive they look on this street, these crowds of colors
Dotted with white. No gray hope, no gray memory,
No dusky signs of lament that they're growing old
Far from the open fields that mothered them
And the forest margins.

The Next Life

If a few more lives are allowed me,
I'd like to give at least one to moving you
From the category of girl whose company I enjoyed
More than the company of others in high school
To the category of heart's companion.

Then I'll be the first person you turn to
When a wave of gloom breaks over you
Like the one that proved too heavy for you to bear.
A gloom I have to suppose on my own
Since only the bare facts reached me, thirdhand,
From a classmate's sister, and almost a year
After you took your life, and you just thirty,
Married, teaching in high school
Just as you'd planned on doing long before.

When I heard, I thought of the story
You wrote for the writing club about a fear
That comes from nowhere to grip the heroine
And then moves off, leaving her shaken. A theme
That seemed surprising for a cheerful girl like you,
So interested in your studies, so popular you could choose
Among those who wanted to be your friend
Just the loyal few you felt at home with.

With me at your side, I let myself imagine,
The dark wave won't hold you under
Long enough to drown you. Holding you up
May take all my skill and stamina
But not more. And when you thank me,
I'll feel I ought to be thanking you
For giving my life an ample purpose,

One I'll point to with pride when anyone asks
What I'm doing to further life on the planet.

As for the life I've chosen this time around,
I wouldn't want to suggest I regret it.
It's just that it seems composed of many little purposes
Not easy to piece together to make a grand one.
Still, though a little lacking in unity and direction,
It's probably one of the dozen or so available
To the boy you knew that should leave him feeling
Grateful for many privileges, whereas your life
Fell short of each of the many that you deserved.

In my rescue project, I help you to one of them.
And when you ask what life I imagine next,
And sketch for me a life much like the one
I'm living now, I say, "No doubt about it,
It's down on my list somewhere, but first I'll rest;
And then I want to live ours again."

Our Death

From the point of view of the dead, it's likely nothing,
As Epicurus argues, but from ours
It's the point on the page where the hand
Writing our story stops moving, no matter
How far the story lies from completion,
And the blank pages ahead are torn away.

The point when friends stop phoning for our opinion
Or to tell us what they always intended to say
But couldn't. And if we imagine a letter then
Placed in our hands, we have to imagine as well
No strength to unfold it, no light to read by
Or to pen an answer with if we had a pen.

Hard to believe the library board meets Tuesday
With us not there to ask why our clients
Still fail to read what we've recommended.
And to think the chairman who seemed to support us
Now recommends that the list we cherished
Be altered to fit the taste of the crowd.

And those still voting our way, listening in the evening
To the discs we left them, will be surprised
At the widening gap between our taste in music
And theirs. And then they'll turn to sketching the plans
For enlarging the summer house we never approved of,
That kept them away from their friends too long.

From a Practical Reader

I'm willing to buy your book of poems
If you can promise that whenever you liken a day
To a coin that can't be hoarded,
You spell out exactly what I should buy with it
In the few hours left me before the sun
Sinks behind the garage outside my window,
What items more valuable than those in the shops,
And mention where they're available locally.

I'm a plain person, I admit, with little patience
For vague suggestions, so if you believe
Poems need to be vague to be suggestive,
I'd better save my money for something else
(Money I don't have endless supplies of,
Not with my job as bookkeeper for a hospital),
A work of history, say, or biography
Or a book of encouragement from the self-help section.

I could use a poem showing that those who seem
To be having a better time at work than I do,
Or a better time at the beach or hiking a trail,
Have simply learned to do more with moods
No better than my good moods,
While making less of the lesser ones.

I won't complain if your book has many poems
Praising the joys of giving so long as it has a few
On the joys of taking. How to choose friends,
For example, who won't forget me after I'm gone,
Who'll tell my story now and then to themselves
If not to others. Friends glad to remember,

Who believe their gladness would be complete
If I were sitting beside them sharing it.

As for friends I've lost, do you have some advice
For the times I'm asked to speak at a funeral
When my feelings, ardent before,
Suddenly seem too cool and measured?
Don't tell me to level my words down
To the flats of fact in the name of integrity
When the task before me is rising to the occasion.
If my feelings can't make the climb, inspire me
To send up some phrases that would be honest
If I were the person I'd like to be.

The Master of Metaphor

Even on days when his body seems too heavy
And broken to live with gracefully,
He tries not to think of it as a prison,
Not to consider himself a spirit
Who merely happens to be embodied.
Better for him, he believes, to begin with body,
Body enlivened, awakened, inspirited.
As for the earth, how can it be a prison
When he's an earthling, his lungs having evolved
To thrive in an atmosphere richly imbued
With the exhalations of earthly plant life,
His legs evolved to carry him to a stand of pear trees,
His arms and hands to reach up and pluck?

And when he wakes in the dark an hour past midnight
With his lungs aching, gasping for breath,
He doesn't blame the weight of his body
Or the weight of the earthly atmosphere.
It's simply the weight of the dark itself.
And when he's tempted to call that dark a prison,
He reminds himself its walls and bars will dissolve
Like mist when dawn finally arrives,
Dear dawn striding across the hills to lift the stone
Night has rolled on his chest and let him rise.
A miracle, he believes he can say without hyperbole,
If the term can refer to familiar splendor,
Not only to what's revealed to the faithful
Far less often than once a day.

Sensible Summers

It isn't absurd to learn the names of the constellations
Visible on a summer night near Wellfleet
So long as you bear in mind they won't learn yours
And you don't presume that your extra learning
Will win the heart of the lovely Lucinda Miles.

Not absurd to mutter her name to yourself
While you paint the porch of your summer house
Pale blue, the color of the heron eggs
You and your brother found in the tall grass
Behind the boathouse when you were boys.
Blue over the hunter green that doubtless
Reminded the man you bought the house from,
Old Mr. Barrows, of an episode even more distant.

The wish to feel the house all yours,
To cast away the awnings and badminton net
That Mr. Barrows stored in the cellar, isn't absurd
So long as you can imagine owners to come
Doing the same one day to your leavings,
Your private papers mattering less to them
Than Barrows' log of the weather matters to you.

Nothing absurd about spending all afternoon
Replacing the punky sections of clapboard
If you don't assume that your side will triumph
In the war with dry rot and damp rot in the years to come,
A war your neighbor appears to have given up.

Tomorrow you'll help him wrestle his boat
Down to the dock for the opening of a season
Delayed two months by an illness that's left him

Bent-backed and sallow. Even if he dies before dawn
He can't be dismissed as absurd for dreaming all night
Of hoisting his sail if he's done it before
In the actual world and never been disappointed.

It isn't absurd to ask if the memory of his boat
Under sail in the harbor isn't just as real
As a boat tacking into the breeze now blowing,
Assuming "real" means available and vivid.
And why not ask, as you sit on the porch
This very evening, how something as small
As the porch can be roomy enough
To contain the husks of all you have left or lost
And the seeds of all you'll be given.

To hope for answers vivid and heartening
Isn't absurd if you recognize their coming
May be delayed while answers far different
Crowd up the walk uninvited
To offer their unremarkable explanations.

Manifesto

Isn't it time, words of the world, to unite?
Time to resolve not to work anymore for the bosses
Who look upon you as so many hands and feet,
Drudges and drones in a garment sweatshop
Turning out coats so rich, so elegant,
They make the ugliest customers appear respectable.

Come gather, words, under the beautiful flag
I'm standing under, after my little stint
With lesser causes, the flag of art.
See how proudly it waves over a workroom
Where the management puts its employees first.
No more crowding together in ill-lit basements.
Each of you will receive the elbow room you deserve
By a bright window that opens on a garden,
Happy in an establishment where means and methods
Are just as important as any end.

"Accept no substitutes." That's the motto
I've sewn in our union logo. "One sentence
Stitched with mindfulness says more than ten
Pasted together to meet a deadline."
And here's a clause in the contract I'm offering
That says whenever you feel weary from overuse
You can take off a month to get your strength back.
No need to worry that some scab of a synonym
Will be smuggled onto the payroll to do your job.

Imagine it, words: not to be asked anymore
To glorify causes you consider shameful
But to praise the beauty that's been neglected,
To draw a map showing it's not remote

But near to anyone willing to do some walking.
A map in your own style, your own inflections
Giving torque to the line or pushing out
Over the line to make room in the sentence
For canyons you won't be asked to fill in,
For knolls you won't be asked to smooth down.

World History

Better to wonder if ten thousand angels
Could waltz on the head of a pin
And not feel crowded than to wonder if now's the time
For the armies of the Austro-Hungarian Empire
To teach the Serbs a lesson they'll never forget
For shooting Archduke Franz Ferdinand in Sarajevo.

Better to go door to door in Düsseldorf or Marseilles
And leave the taxpayers scratching their heads
At your vague report of a kingdom within
Than argue it's time for Germany to display
A natural love for its Austrian kin, or time
For France to make good on its pledge to Russia,
Or time for England to honor its word to France
Or give up thinking itself a gentleman.

To wonder, after a month without one convert,
If other people exist, if they share the world
That you inhabit, if you've merely dreamed them
To keep from feeling lonely—that's enough
To make the silence that falls when your words give out
A valley of shadows you fear to pass through.
But it can't compare to the silence of bristling nations
Standing toe to toe in a field, each army certain
It couldn't be anywhere else, given the need
Of great nations to be ready for great encounters.

And if it's hard to believe that spirit
Is anything more than a word when defined
As something separate from what is mortal,
It's easy to recognize the spirit of the recruit
Not convinced his honor has been offended

Who decides it's time to step from the line
And catch a train back to his cottage
Deep in the boondocks, where his wife and daughter
Are waiting to serve him supper and hear the news.

The Actor

He doesn't deny that confessing his limitations
Might serve as a useful prologue to moving forward,
Just not so useful as pretending to be accomplished.
On his list of virtues, ambition outranks sincerity.
It doesn't matter how unpracticed he is
So long as he plays the part he chooses
As he imagines a great actor might play it.
It doesn't matter if the robe he borrows
Drags in the sawdust and his wooden sword
Jostles the table as he bends to outline,
On a fake map of a kingdom, his towns and forests.
Wanting to be a forester, he enters a forest.
Coming upon a river, he finds a canoe
And paddles off as if he knows what he's doing.
When it tips as he turns, he pretends he can swim,
And soon he's crawling ashore, winded,
To rest in the sun as his mother and father
Told him to rest after exertion
Back when they were playing the part of parents
More convincingly than they did when first
It was thrust upon them. Then it joined
Their ensemble of other impersonations
Practiced till all looked easy, carried off
With the kind of grace that deserves commending.
If their son acts like he's happy to praise them
Often enough, however stingy he may be feeling,
He'll be generous, according to his convictions,
Worthy of admiration from everyone;
Forced admiration, maybe, at first; then natural.

Dream Theory

Not every dream I wake from
Leaves me feeling uneasy.
Some are wishes pure and simple
That pass through customs unmolested.

My dream last night about traveling
With Lynne in Europe seemed to express
A wish uncompromised by the clamor of fact.
The thirty-year gap between the present
And the era in which I failed to persuade her
I was her destiny was an inch-wide crack
For my feelings to skip across
As they charged the gangway
With all our luggage, off for a voyage
We didn't manage to take before.

All those with degrees in dream analysis
Are free to turn for the day to the harder problems
That social workers and teachers are up against.
In my dream the reality principle
Showed merely as gray streaks in her hair
And a few wrinkles that seemed becoming.
Reality made us linger so long in Mantua
Over pumpkin pasta, sharing the inside story
About the Renaissance,
That we almost missed our train to Verona.

The only painful part of the dream
Was leaving her at a mountain hotel
When I went to Paris to lecture on the Bastille
That poetry sometimes opens. But soon I returned
To find her standing alone on the terrace,

Her face lit by a smile that anyone
Skilled in interpreting smiles would say
Showed how happy she felt that moment,
How lucky. And when I woke I marveled
How lightly the weight of history
Presses on a sleeper's chest as he dreams.

It's likely the muscle that pumps the blood
Finds the work a little harder each year,
But it still seems eager to pound if a name is mentioned
Or a letter that fails to arrive is imagined
Waiting among the magazines and the catalogues.

So what if the signature and the date are missing
And the paper's so yellowed and wrinkled
I have to step to the window to read it.
"That hand," the heart says stoutly,
"I'd know it anywhere."

Candles

If on your grandmother's birthday you burn a candle
To honor her memory, you might think of burning an extra
To honor the memory of someone who never met her,
A man who may have come to the town she lived in
Looking for work and couldn't find it.
Picture him taking a stroll one morning,
After a wasted month with the want ads,
To refresh himself in the park before moving on.
Suppose he notices on the gravel path the shards
Of a green glass bottle that your grandmother,
Then still a girl, will be destined to step on
When she wanders barefoot away from her school picnic
If he doesn't stoop down and scoop the mess up
With the want-ad section and carry it to a trash can.

For you to burn a candle for him
You needn't suppose the cut would be a deep one,
Just deep enough to keep her at home
The night of the hayride when she meets Helen,
Who is soon to become her dearest friend;
Whose brother George, thirty years later,
Helps your grandfather with a loan so his shoe store
Doesn't go under in the Great Depression
And his son, your father, is able to stay in school
Where his love of learning is fanned into flames,
A love he labors, later, to kindle in you.

How grateful you are for your father's efforts
Is shown by the candles you've burned for him.
But today, for a change, why not a candle
For the man whose name is unknown to you?
Take a moment to wonder whether he died at home

With friends and family or alone on the road,
With no one to sit at his bedside
And hold his hand, the very hand
It's time for you to imagine holding.

from

A House of My Own

(1974)

Useful Advice

Suppose you sat writing at your desk
Between days, long before dawn,
The only one up in town,
And suddenly saw out the window
A great star float by,
Or heard on the radio sweet voices
From wandering Venus or Neptune,
A little hello from the voids.
Who would believe you in the morning
Unless you'd practiced for years
A convincing style?
So you must learn to labor each day.
Finally a reader may write he's certain
Whatever you've written or will write is true.
Then all you need is the patience to wait
For stars or voices.

Students

A middle-aged man inspects the painting
That seems to present a boy with a bird and a whale.
Though his children, perhaps, have refused his counsel,
Though his wife has a lover who borrows money,
And his job at the savings-and-loan isn't inspiring,
He lays no blame on his country's decline,
Or his mother's coldness, or the slope of his chin,
But humbly supposes his ignorance does him in.
So he looks hard at the painted scene.
Maybe the boy with the bird and the whale
Would tell him something useful about the soul
If only he hadn't neglected his studies.
He needs a teacher, he thinks, to help him see,
And looking around the room discovers me
Looking at him with my sympathetic stare.
If he comes this way, I'll have to tell him the truth
About the shortage of teachers everywhere.

Relatives

"Remember your father the wolf,"
The lecturer says.
"Chewed by its appetite it chews its prey.
It howls with fear in the woods
Beyond blame or praise.
Drop food in your children's cages
When they follow commands,
And they'll all be good."

During the lecture, it was later learned,
Crows were observed tumbling in loops
Over North Dakota.
Two dogs at leisure on a beach in France
Ran a race to a rock.
In the Indian Ocean
Thirty leagues down
Men in a diving bell picked up an hour's aria
From a pod of whales in a language unknown
Sung to unknown listeners leagues away.

Remember your old cousins,
Those fish who crawled from the sea
When seafood was plentiful
And the land bare.
Think of the voices they strained to hear
As they chose to hobble on tender fins
Painfully in the sun's glare.

Knots

I respect your plan to slip into the graveyard
One of these nights and topple your father's stone
And dance on your mother's grave
To the tune of your old grudge.
One night while you were sleeping,
They crept into your little attic room
And tied all the furniture to the floor.
So you spend your life untying knots,
The slowest work of all. And every morning,
After a night spent dreaming of rearrangements,
You wake up to find it all roped down again.

Still, you might picture brave young sailors,
As they boomed along in a gale off Cape Horn
With creaking spars and strained lashings,
Thanking their lucky stars for the bowline,
That ingenious knot passed down for so many years
From old sailors to young
With care, with patience.

from
Climbing Down
(1976)

Ingratitude

Spring, I remembered you all these months.
I spoke of the green yard under the snow
To my slumped visitors.
I sobered the giddy neighbors.
"You may think you're still happy,"
I cautioned, "but recall the tea roses,
The lost leaves of the dogwood tree."

But now you have fallen upon us, Spring,
Without warning,
So much greener than I remembered.
Friends I kept from forgetting
Laugh at me as they run outside
For falling so short in your praise.

The Homeowner

When I turn the key, I like to hear the furniture
Straightening up for inspection,
Poising expectantly in the hush.
Sometimes a few pieces aren't ready
And it seems I intrude on the couch and chair
Or startle the lamp-table from a nap;
But most often they show me courtesy.

It's my pictures that ignore me—
The girl holding a rose to the light,
The fisherman drifting alone in his rowboat,
The couple strolling a woodland path.
I stand a foot from their frames and wait;
With gestures I invite their confidence;
But they hold aloof, too distant to nod,
Too proud to acknowledge an audience.

They're in love with their own weather for good.
They need no comments of mine
To sweeten life in their walled preserve.
They gladly will me my furniture and its deference,
All things that pass through the house
On the outside.

The Peaceable Kingdom

No rust on the fenders but the car won't start.
You tear open the hood and stare in.
The fuel pump's clogged with flowers.
You suspect mischief, but the old enemy
Spring infects everything.
The engine block is all thumbs
As it daydreams of colliding hard
With the shapely Pontiac
Parked down the block.
Give up. Take a walk.
Pull the tail of your two-tone collie.
Pull the hair of your idling girlfriend.
Your old road plans have been suspended.

Praise for My Heart

Don't you deserve a few lines for youself,
You who work in the dark, in silence,
Under no orders, with no weekends free,
Shipping food to the hungry cells
On all my peripheries?
When I wake in the morning it seems clear
You've been at it all night
I get up shamed by your diligence.

What can such effort signify
But faith in the enterprise?
You're certain the world would be wounded
If you once failed me.
You believe in me without thinking.

Native Son

You try to imagine highways to all men
But your heart has always loved boundaries,
The heavy fields in back of your house,
The visible streets of America.

Now when a plane crashes in Paris
You scan the death list for American names,
And only when American gunners fly out
Do you board the plane in your dream
And jostle the pilots, and grab the controls.

America is your friend at a loud party.
Her jokes are no worse than the others
But they sadden you most.
You want to take her home before it's too late.

It's hard to write letters in your attic study
When you hear your father downstairs
Smashing the furniture on his path to a glass.
He was a wino before you were born;
You are not to blame,
You say to yourself as you go down
To look at the mess.

from
Signs and Wonders
(1979)

Listeners

After midnight, when I phone up a far-off friend
To describe my chills or a blister by the heart
That won't wait, I can hear the breath of the operator
As she listens in, lonely among the night wires.
They all do it, breaking the rules.
In the morning she takes home my story to her husband, her
    friends.
A sad burden. No useful wisdom yet.
No advice about selling the house, the move to Florida,
The right neighborhood for the boys.

It's getting harder to tell where the words go.
You send them off with instructions not to stop on the road,
Not to speak to strangers, but as they run they spill over.
Even on a bare bench when you whisper to yourself,
Sigh softly how the world has let you down,
From the bench in back you can hear a breath.
Your thoughts have entered the far world;
They have changed to stones;
And someone walks round them as he climbs.

Near Idaville

Has the story reached you of those few who live alone
And love it, and never open their mail?
The long Sahara of summer vacation is for them a sea.
They put forth boldly on billowy mornings,
Crowd sail through fragrant nights when no one knocks,
Free at last for their mission to rewrite
The history of the world in a room
Near Idaville, in back of the drygoods store.
Hunched by the lamp, each asks a question of himself;
Each listens thoughtfully to his own replies.
Wiser than before, he jots them down.
In his one-man apartment a quiet pair,
A lifetime of dialogue.

How far away this life is from your solitude.
For always on your hunting trip to the North,
In your rented cabin, at the edge of the pines,
With a wide prospect of the valley, you hope for visitors,
And imagine a couple beside you sharing the view.
And they, your own creations, though they love the quiet,
Want visitors too, and dream of the field
Filled with strangers who look like friends, but happier,
A congenial race of enlightened souls
Walking arm in arm in graceful pairs
Slowly along the hills and down,
Greeting each other with warm, ceremonious smiles.

And you imagine them too, and wait for them.
And you're sure whoever hopes for their company
Deserves to be loved not for himself or his work
But for his endless need to become like them,

These strangers who are not yet here,
Whose bones, though beautiful and sure to endure,
Are thin as light and light as air.

Carpentry

Carpenters whose wives have run off
Are sometimes discovered weeping on the job.
But even then they don't complain of their work.

Whitman's father was a carpenter.
He was so happy hammering houses
That he jumped with a shout from the roof beam
And rolled with a yawp in the timothy.
This led his son to conclude wrongly
That all workmen are singers.

Whitman's father was weak.
He had trouble holding a job.
He hoped that the house he was working on
Would be lived in by a man more steady
Than he was, who would earn his sleep,
Dreaming easy under a sound roof
With no rain in his face.

Of course, there are bad carpenters everywhere.
They don't care if the walls don't meet.
"After all," they argue,
"We're not building airplanes."
But Whitman's father measured his nails.
Many mornings, clacking his plane,
He crooned a song to the corners,
Urging them on to a snug fit.
No needles of heat will escape through a crack
If he can help it, no threads of light.

Snow

Thirty-four years haven't put a dent
In my vision of snowstorms, my impatience
With the paltry inches of the winter dole,
Slim pickings even in Buffalo.
My hunger is to wake in the morning
In the deep dark, the windows snowed over,
The doors opening into walls. No one can move.
Nothing to do but tunnel. So I push out
With my snow shovel, clearing a dark hall
To the buried toolshed, quieting my rabbits
And spaniels, who feed from my hand.
Then I turn to rescue my neighbors, the near
And the far, pausing to relieve the drugstore,
Helping the weeping pharmacist from behind the counter.
He offers me medicine for a lifetime, which I refuse.
I dig to uncover roofs and porches.
At every door I leave frozen breadloaves,
Pound with stone fists, and hurry away,
Too busy to wait for an introduction.
The hungry families spend hours in vain
Guessing the name of their deliverer.

The Tree

Only the outermost ring of the tree you love
Is alive. All trees are like that,
The spine wholly dead
And the dead wood undecayed,
Bracing the sap-flow just under the bark.
Slowly the sap edges up
When the daylight is long enough
And the leaves unfurl for their outdoor work.

Far below your surface, the tree inside you
Scratches as it sways in the night wind,
Knocks its branches in the dark under the ribs.
It's hard to tell where its roots are bedded,
What clear pool it's groping for;
Hard to know if it's nourished
When you walk out under the stars
Or read late by the fire.
If it dies it dies from within,
Withers and rots to nothing, and you live on
Afraid of the wind,
Branches scattered on the ground,
The hollow trunk filling up with leaves.

Sunday

In the fading photograph of the pleasure boat
The pleasure-seekers, dressed in their Sunday best,
Crowd all three decks, women in sun hats
Pausing to chat with bearded men in derbies
Who lean on the rail, listening to the band.

On shore, the quiet farms slide by. Here and there
A cluster of low houses, a river town. The sun
Shines overhead. Everyone looks willing to be interested,
Pointing to the inlets and islands, recalling their names,
Though many have boarded the boat nudged by a friend,
By a promise to a child, though the children are already lost,
Crying with their dolls in the passageways.

It's only because they're long dead
That they all look sad. But some must be happy.
Some must refuse to envy the boats in front
Or look back on the boats behind and sigh.
The ride is no empty promise to them
Of a better ride to come, and no omen of a worse.
Whatever they expected to be shown is here.

Whatever lies behind the water, the sun, the air,
The uniforms of the band, is too imperfect to be seen,
Unfinished, still composing its face in the dark,
Waiting, as this moment waited, below deck
Till the Sunday comes when it's ready to appear.

Grandmother and I

Grandmother sits on the couch in our tiny apartment
Over the drugstore, leafing through the news.
She's larger than my parents and knows all things.
It's turning out just as she expected.
The same hoodlums are climbing on the trains
And buying up all the seats.
"You don't have to read the paper to learn this,"
She mutters to herself, and nods.

When I come to the couch for a story
She bends down and whispers, slightly deaf,
"Obey your father." Her voice is warm.
Such phrases in her Russian accent often mean, "Young man,
How are you today, whoever you are?
Where are you going in your cowboy suit?"

We don't expect her to remember all our names.
By middle age she'd outlived five presidents
And the sons of two czars.
Napoleon himself, it's rumored, as he neared the border,
Stopped at Grandmother's for advice.
"You'll be sorry, Napoleon," she said;
"Go home and stay warm."
It's hard to convince an emperor.

Many have grown small with the years,
But every year Grandmother grows larger,
Like a tree by sweet water.
The whole family sleeps without fear
In the widening circle of her shade.

At night in my bed,
Groping my way in dream through cloudy streets,
I hear from her branches far above
Birds that sing of the workshop of my father,
Boris the long-lost tailor, still alive,
Waiting in the story I've always loved.

A Plea for More Time

New Year's already come and gone
And the wish still miles away
To live here again;

To be cast up after an interval
Back to this yard, the same man,
No heaven or hell between,

Immortal return to the lumberpile.
After sweating out new plans for a table
To build the old one again.

So little time left, and still
Nothing I've won would make me glad
To win it forever;

To notice a mirror face at the window
With lines I'd weep to alter,
Like the face of a friend.

And to think of walking the night rounds
Full of love for my gatelocks,
Blessing the knots of boundary wire

And the hills behind blocking my view;
How strangely slow the watchman saunters;
How far away he seems even now.

The Band

Pensioners fondle the books in the sidewalk bins
For the big bargains, two for a dollar:
Eat Yourself Slim, Secret Missions of the Civil War,
Great Train Wrecks, Photographing Your Dog.
At home on their tables the books, never finished, pile up,
Their promises not fulfilled. The pensioners pace in their rooms.

Sundays they're called outside by the music of the band
From the green rotunda. The musicians strain at their horns.
Their necks are pinched by the starched collars of their uniforms.
They appear to be playing in this heat from duty,
As if asked by friends. Others may enjoy the music
If not them, so why not play for an afternoon?

The music floats up and away over the roofs
To the window of your hilltop room, where you lie in bed,
Whispering to your one love.
All morning you've played together slowly and quietly,
Free of the need to rush to some grand finale
That drives the strivers in the town,
The young attorneys, who crave release.

Over this ample district of the present
Floats the mournful, dowdy music of the band.
It mingles with your sighs as you rise to dress.
You move with its rhythms to the straight-back chair at your desk
Where your paper lies ready, forms for a new agreement
Between you and the town, between the town and your one love

As she steps outside to mingle with the pensioners,
Who listen patiently to the band,

Hoping if they stay to the end
That something left behind in their rooms
Won't look the same when they return.

from

The Near World

(1985)

Hector's Return

By now he's died so often
And been dragged in the dirt so many times
It's easy. He'd have it no other way
And chooses with open eyes
To be deluded by his will to live
And press the attack on the ships,
To forget what he knew at the opening,
That Troy must burn, abandoned by its gods,
His wife and son doomed to be slaves,
His name lost among strangers.

It hurts me to see his mistaken hope,
Though I'm glad that the man I left last year
As ashes cooling on a funeral pyre
Has risen long enough
To fight Achilles once again and fall.
A poem that shows the generations of men
As frail as the generations of leaves,
That makes my solid city flutter in the wind
Like Troy and thin to shadows, as unreal
As my grandmother's village in Lithuania,
Burned down in the War,
Or as the farm she lived on here,
Paved over for a mall years back,
Is the same poem that's watered roses
In Priam's garden so they bloom still.
I turn the page and the trampled leaves
Float up again to the branches
And turn green. And it seems for a moment
That time is too weak a god to worship,

Another illusion I can put my hand through,
Not the last word, as I supposed.

We assumed Grandmother's muttering at the end
About waves and crossings
To be her dream of some longed-for,
Fabled afterworld,
Not guessing she was a girl again
Crossing the sea to us,
Eager to rejoin the long line
On Ellis Island.

At the Corner

This slender woman in the rain, rounding the corner,
Looks too determined for a trip to the store.
Maybe she turned on her porch a few moments before
And called back a few reminders to the baby-sitter—
If anyone calls, she's shopping up the block—
Then hurried the other way. Now she's half done
With her journey crosstown to the tenements.
I can see her later as she climbs four flights
And lets herself in with her key.
In the tiny room, dim beneath a bare bulb,
Her friend lies huddled in bed, coughing,
His face to the wall. Without a word
She clears a space at the littered table
And washes two mugs at the sink for tea.

For an hour they discuss the real questions.
Is spirit unfolding itself slowly in history,
As Hegel argues, or holding back,
Camping out all year in open fields?
And why is spirit missing in the new novel
The woman recounts to her friend this week?
It makes her sad to meet characters not permitted
To think for themselves, who have to make do
With reciting, when asked, a few dull proverbs.

The man sipping tea at the table agrees.
He sketches the plot of the fable he's working on,
The Mermaid and the Carpenter, how the two
Meet on the dock, exchange a few words on the weather,
And suddenly love. Imagine the obstacles.

The woman tries to picture their house by the sea
As she walks home later,
Certain their blueprints can be reconciled.
And now the house floats into focus, its stilts and piers.
The way there seems nearly as clear
As the way this tree on the corner, shining in the rain,
Calls up for me a long walk in the rain
With someone I believe was you.

The Midlands

In summer in our town,
When the ghost of Hamlet's father, stifled,
Wrenches from his grave, lunges up the road
Toward the hillside cabin of his son, the stargazer,
Perched higher than the goats graze,
He tires halfway and sits down, panting, on a stone.
In the town below the streetlamps glitter.
The street noise thins to nothing as it climbs.
Listen as he might, he hears no cries of revenge
Among all the scraping of crickets and leaves.
After an hour what can he do but head home?
Meanwhile his son, undistracted, his eyes on the stars,
Hauls his blanket to the roof for a clearer picture,
Jots down his sightings, dozes off at dawn.

In winter in our town,
When white-haired wise men arrive
With handmade presents for the child,
They get lost in a bad district and are robbed.
It's snowing hard when they try to rise.
They stagger to the lighted door of the bar.
The barkeeper washes their wounds.
In the morning, waking in a beer haze,
They're too ashamed to go on.
So the child, never named, grows up ignorant
And copies the habits of his friends,
Tries to be last inside when his mother calls,
Jockeys for first place in line on the Sabbath
At the double doors of the Tivoli,
Whose double feature never seems to change.

Beauty Exposed

At the bookstore you wait for the new clerk,
The beautiful one, who sold the books you ordered
To someone else, though the plain one
Brings you what you need unasked.

Not wanting to feel guilt, the Greeks
Made beauty the gift of a goddess,
Called their love for fine features piety.
And Plato, straining to prove man rational,
Argued that to love the beautiful
As all men do is to love the good,
The two one in the spectral world
Of metaphor, where the question's begged.
Here where we live, in the cave,
Nobody's fooled.

And nobody's foolish enough to believe
It lives only in the beholder, as personal
As your taste for the ginger cookies
Your mother made, which no one else liked.
Too much agreement for that and for too long.
The statues in the museum aren't exchanged
Each year for new ones. They stay,
And we find new reasons, new ways to explain
Why they wake the flesh in the old way.

All our heads turned in unison
When the girl in the blue dress entered
And walked along the library aisles
To the section on law and kneeled
Or stood on her toes, hair flung back.
Before she uttered a word we could look behind,

Before an action we could dream up motives for,
We had to sit confounded by the surface glare
Of the visible, frightened to be so far
From the dark world we understand.

Captain Cook

So often had he sailed the world in dream
That even the first voyage was more like homage
To the gods of repetition than like discovery.

The day the land birds perched in the spars
After months of empty seas was one of many.
Again through mist the steep headland
Or the same flat beach at dawn when the sky cleared
Or darkened. Always the excited crowds on shore,
The flotilla of canoes, the eager swimmers,
Young men and girls laughing among the ropes.

Today he may call their home New Zealand,
Tomorrow the Society Islands or Friendly Islands.
And this is Mercury Bay, Hawke Bay, or Bream Bay.
Time again for patching the wound in the main keel,
For refilling the water casks and exchanging cloth and nails
For pigs and fruit, rock oysters and yams.

Always the same trouble with island thieves,
The spyglass missing again, the quadrant, the anchor buoys,
More shovels, pulleys, bolts, and screws,
Till the worst offenders are driven off with small shot
Or flogged, and the sailors are flogged again
For not stowing their muskets more carefully.

Today as before the Captain rows after two deserters
And climbs the hill to their leafy hideaway
And drags them from the arms of the weeping island girls

Back to the ship, and again the sailors wail
Like Odysseus's sailors dragged back from the lotus fields.

And now a chief rows out to deliver his long,
Incomprehensible speech of welcome,
And the Captain, like a man who's been everywhere,
Patiently hears him out to the end,
Then makes his own incomprehensible speech in return
And proceeds to the rubbing of noses, as is the custom.

Not a part of all he meets, not hungry for experience,
Though no one is readier when it comes to tasting
The boiled South-Sea dog and the worm stew,
No one more impressed by the nightlong paddle dance.
It doesn't matter to him how much or little his heart
Is written on by adventure as he writes in his log
His reckoning of the latitude, practicing the same skill
He practiced before in the same Pacific
Under the moon in its numbered phases
And the wheel of stars.

At Home with Cézanne

When the phone rings down the hall, I let it ring.
I sit still in my study chair and go on reading
About Cézanne. Sarah will answer it.
Most likely it's for her, an old boyfriend
From high school, or her first husband,
Calling for more advice, attentive still.

Only this evening I learned that Zola and Cézanne
Grew up together in Aix-en-Provence,
Friends through their boyhood and beyond.
What a great log of a fact
To throw on an autumn fire and muse on
When my books grow dull, to think what encouragement
Passed between them on their daylong rambles.

Why should I worry if her heart is large enough
For them all? I should be proud
To hear her voice through the wall
Grow sad when the caller's voice grows sad
Or brighten as his brightens.

Though Cézanne in Paris found few friends
To be open with, he found a tribe of painters
To learn from, and that was enough,
The silent encouragement of high examples.

She'd tell me who the callers are
If I ever asked her.
Why should I sift the soil

If her roots sink deep enough
And the tree is flourishing?

It's too dark to see from my window
The dogwood we planted this year.
The breeze lifting the curtains
Carries the smell of dry leaves
Fallen on a street in Paris outside the Salon.
Zola and Cézanne are glad to walk out of there
And breathe the fresh air of fall.
They're not surprised that the judges
Threw out all the entries that were dazzling.

Now as the smell of leaves reaches her room
She may recall, as she listens,
Walking with me last fall. It's not unlikely,
But why begrudge her an earlier memory?
Let her go riding again on her father's farm,
Bouncing along on a pony she's never mentioned,
Who wouldn't be fed by anyone but her.

More Music

This one thinks he's lucky when his car
Flips over in the gully and he climbs out
With no bones broken, dusts himself off,
And walks away, eager to forget the episode.

And this one when her fever breaks
And she opens her eyes to breeze-blown,
Sky-blue curtains in a sunlit house
With much of her life still before her
And nothing she's done too far behind her
To be called back, or remedied, or atoned.

Now she'll be glad to offer her favorite evening hours
To Uncle Victor and listen as he tells again
How the road washed out in the rain
And he never made it to Green Haven in time
To hear the Silver Stars and the Five Aces.
And she'll be glad to agree that the good bands
Lift the tunes he likes best above them to another life,
And agree it isn't practice alone
That makes them sound that way
But luck, or something better yet.

And if Victor thinks he's a lucky man for the talk
And for his room in his nephew's house
Up beneath the rafters, and the sweet sound of the rain
Tapping on the tar paper or ringing in the coffee can,
Should we try to deny it? Why make a list
Of all we think he's deserved and missed
As if we knew someone to present it to
Or what to say when told we're dreaming
Of an end unpromised and impossible,
Unmindful of the middle, where we all live now?

What Has Become of Them

Somewhere back in the lost place, you're still repeating
The same partial, uninspired replies to the girl
Who looks out the diner window in despair,
And your mother still wipes her eyes, still walks away
From the grave of her daughter,
And your dead father still searches for a house
Where bad thoughts can't force the door.

Once you thought these ventures finished,
Crumbled to powder, blown away. Now you know
They go on elsewhere as they were, unheard, invisible,
As the stream found in the woods, breaking on the rocks
In white water, continues to break after you've gone.

The sea wall washes away; the tree blows down
In the summer storm. But you still wake in the house
That burned to the ground years back
And turn to the arms of your young wife
In fresh joy, as if the fire were merely dreamed.

These moments are far now, farther each day,
But at night you make it to the town they live in
And watch them at their lighted windows
As they lose themselves in their parts
With the same emphatic gestures,
Not one word altered, not one left out.
They're too caught up to notice their audience,
And it doesn't matter if you stay to watch
Or drift to the spectral outskirts of tomorrow.

Later

Later you'll notice how slanted the floors are
And learn the meaning of the cracks above the lintels.
Now on the morning you move in
The dazzling, eastern light floods the big rooms.
The man who couldn't be happy here
Under these high ceilings won't find another place.

If you saw now what you'll see then
You wouldn't be moving in, though later
You won't regret your choice.
The bad news will arrive slowly and be different,
Not like a stranger's illness but a friend's.
You'll sit by his bed to cheer him up.

Then it's back to your study
To finish your novel about the lake.
Later you'll see how coarse it is,
Not the last draft, as you suppose now,
But the first. Be grateful for your ignorance,
For the gift of foolish confidence that allows you to begin.

On the first day out with his new boat,
Your hero, docking on an island,
Meets a stranger down on his luck
And invites him home.
Later, when he pulls in the driveway,
You can have him remember how small his house is,
How crammed with relatives,
All of them fretful as the years
Rub them the wrong way.

For now, as the breeze bellies the sails,
Let him imagine guest rooms waiting, and guest wings,
And months left at the doors like gifts,
May baskets, June boxes, July crowns,
August horns of plenty.

Charity

Time to believe that the thin disguise
On the face of the blessing in disguise
Will never be pulled off,

That the truth that's still in hiding
Will stay there, far in the dark.
All that can be revealed is revealed.

All that can be learned from the burning house
Was learned the first time, when the smoke
Blackened the walls in every room.

So much for more experience. What can grow
Has grown; what's small now stays small.
No portion waits for those who deserve more.

The flowers in the yard of the blind and deaf girl
Will never smell any sweeter to her
Than they smell now to any of her visitors.

The music she imagines will never compare to ours.
Her best day will brighten with no joy
That hasn't brightened our day more.

Time to admit that her steady cheer
Is the burden she assumes to keep us here
Touching her fingers for a while.

Time Heals All Wounds

The first wound, the cut at the cord stem,
No longer tender, the scab fallen off,
The baby no longer sleeping with its knees
Tucked up, dreaming of the dark,
But reaching for the window on belly,
Elbows, and hands, on feeble frog legs;

The cut closed in the boy's head
Received as he ran back for the catch,
Not hearing as the fielder called for it
Or hearing but not believing the ball
Destined for anyone but him;

Pain gone from the wrist
Sprained when the enemy stormed the camp
And tore the flag from the guard's hands
While the guard played dead,
Thinking how unfair it was
For the good side to be so outnumbered;

The tear in the hollow of the thigh
Where the angel touched it and the holy,
Aspiring sap of the wrestler
Leaked out, wetting the ground,
Feeding the seed of a flower whose smell
No one alive remembers, all healed now;

The wounds in the back
Where once the wings joined the body
Healed, and the legs grown used
To the whole weight.

from

The Outskirts of Troy

(1988)

Heinrich Schliemann

If the main plot in his life were his rise
From grocer's apprentice and shipwrecked scrivener
To rich indigo merchant with a palace in St. Petersburg,
The master of a dozen languages, it would be easy
For critics like us to patronize,
Easy to grant him a place in the storybook
With Dick Whittington and the woodcutter's youngest son.
And we could pity his distance from the real world
When he leaves the trading firm in middle age
To learn the ancient Greek of Homer
And falls in love with an Athenian schoolgirl
When he hears her recite Andromache's long plea
And marries her, moving his life from storybook
Into dream, as if the noise of traffic outside the church
Were the hubbub on the fields around Troy.

If only he hadn't taken it into his head
To dig in a sleepy backwater village
For Troy's walls and somehow found them;
If he hadn't knelt in the dirt all day
With beautiful Sophia, chipping away crust
From the tiles of Priam's palace, from bracelets
That once circled the slim wrists of princesses;
If he hadn't proved that his dream was graspable,
That the stories he loved were fashioned in the high style
Not to escape the world but to remember it,
An offering to the dead, to the dead bright ones
Whose gestures, vivid as they are in song,
Were doubtless in the flesh more dazzling.

The Promised Land

The land of Israel my mother loves
Gets by without the luxury of existence
And still wins followers,
Though it can't be found on the map
West of Jordan or south of Lebanon,
Though what can be found bears the same name,
Making for confusion.

Not the land I fought her about for years
But the one untarnished by the smoke of history,
Where no one informs the people of Hebron or Jericho
They're squatting on property that isn't theirs,
Where every settler can remember wandering.

The dinners I spoiled with shouting
Could have been saved,
Both of us lingering quietly in our chairs,
If I'd guessed the truth that now is obvious,
That she wasn't lavishing all her love
On the country that doesn't deserve so rich a gift
But on the one that does, the one not there,
That she hoped good news would reach its borders

And cross into the land of the righteous and merciful
That the Prophets spoke of in their hopeful moods,
That was loved by the red-eyed rabbis of Galicia
Who studied every word of the book and prayed
To get one thread of the meaning right;
The Promised Land where the great and small
Hurry to school and the wise are waiting.

Henry James and Hester Street

Two or three characters talking in a lamplit parlor
Beside a fire, the curtains closed—
So the novel begins, and James is happy.
What a relief to reach this quiet shelter,
Back from America, far from the castles of Fifth Avenue,
From their fresh, unweathered vulgarity,
Far from change run wild, the past trundled away,
His father's dependable neighborhood
Forced to give ground to "glazed perpendiculars"
That compel the passersby to feel equal, equally small.

In the curtained parlor, where tea is being served,
The banker protagonist fills the cups so graciously
I'm convinced he's gathered his treasure with spotless hands,
His flaws as fine as the hairline cracks
In the landscapes from the Renaissance that adorn the walls.
Why shouldn't James protect his characters from the world
If that's what he thinks they need to be free?
Soon they'll have problems enough of their own
Without being made to feel what their maker felt
Touring Manhattan slums, shoved to the curb
By hordes of "ubiquitous aliens." Imagine those crowds
Hawking and bargaining on Hester Street,
Their clanging pushcarts and swarming children,
Immigrants like the couple in the photograph in my hall,
My mother's father and mother fresh off the boat.
Had I stood where James stood back then
They'd have made me uneasy too,
Though now I assume they felt even more alien
Than James felt when he left for good.

As the banker, setting his cup down,
Peers at a landscape to inspect some travelers
Sheltered under a plane tree in a storm,
I inspect the faces in the photograph
As they stare out, eager and sober,
Brave though confused. Their faith in a life
Whose outlines even now are still concealed
Inspires me, just as James's fidelity to his muse
Must have inspired the younger writers who visited.
Pulling their coats on, they stepped out into the chill
And grimy fog they planned to describe in plainer,
Ruder detail, but in a light more revealing
Than the murky light of history, the day more meaningful
Than any November Tuesday in 1913.

Visiting a Friend Near Sagamon Hill

If I take this drive as leisurely as I can,
I may remember, by the time I spot my friend's house,
My speech of consolation,
Which so far seems to have hidden itself
Among the speeches powerless to console,
The ones that silence would be an improvement on.

This road winding through beech and sycamore,
This spring sunlight filtered and shimmering,
Reminds me I'm one of the lucky few.
I too have grown on well-drained soil
In unstinted sun, smiled on,
As Homer might say, by Hyperion,
Not like the stunted, scrubby trees
Rooting below in marshland.

Those marsh trees are like my sick friend,
Whose life hasn't been sent to test him
But to sap him, to wear him down.
One life, and he knows that his one hope now
Is to be two people,
The sufferer and the one who observes
His suffering from above
As calmly as Zeus observes from grassy Ida
The warriors fighting and falling at Troy,
At ease in the best seat in the house.
That's it, down there, the little dark spot
Balancing the highlights on the other side.

The scene lingers a moment and then fades.
Zeus drifts back to the clouds;
My friend discovers himself in bed

Listening as a car crunches in the gravel drive.
Now for the task of finding himself delighted
When his visitor tells him the road from the valley floor
Has never looked greener, the beech and sycamore
Escaped from the clutch of winter without a scratch.

Twenty Years

I

Other prisoners you've written to
Must have told you stories like mine,
How, when they were ten or eleven,
Their fathers began to drink too much,
How when the beatings grew too heavy
They ran loose all night.

I'm willing to admit that my brothers, as wild as I was,
Turned out all right. I don't compare
Their daily killings on the market now
With the one killing on my hands.

All I ask you to see is how much more hate
I had to keep in check than you had to
Or have to now, how good feelings,
When they come to you, come mostly from the heart,
Unforced, not from the will.
If I could write well
I'd write a book on the subject of unequal chances,
Unequal tests and trials,
And not mention myself at all.

The subject must interest you too.
Why else would you want to write me,
A stranger and a prisoner? I'm glad you do
In spite of the days when a bad taste rises in my throat
As I think how little anger you have to swallow
Waking each day in the sunlit, carpeted room
I imagine you waking in.
It's a full day's work for me not to envy

Your lack of envy for any man
As you look down on your garden.

In my best daydream I see myself down there
Talking with your friends, nodding and laughing.
I'm cheering on a friendly game of croquet
And want to join in, but don't,
Afraid that the mallet in my hands
Might turn out dangerous, a missed shot
Stirring up something dark from the bottom
That for years had been slowly settling
Because I'd been holding my life still.

II

Now that they're sleeping,
Their radios still till dawn,
I'm alone with the thin wedge of stars
Visible from the high window.
I have time to name all the clusters I can,
Trying to move with them as they shift west
Over land I want to know more of,
Old free states and slave,
Indian settlements, abandoned mining camps.

The more I learn, the more I feel wasted here
And the lonelier, angry at the many
Not angered by their ignorance,
Then angry at myself for vanity.
Why should they want to study
When the only student they know
Is far more sullen than they are

And aging faster, gray as a ghost,
The thinnest shadow in the land of shadows.

III

Yesterday wind seemed to be blowing
Out through the open gate of the garden
I try to believe in,
The one I carry with me.
I could almost smell the trees blossoming.
And it seemed that nothing here could hurt me.
Whatever happened would leave me strong,
Whatever time did or the guards.
And the guards seemed human,
Even the worst ones, more afraid than cruel.

So if today the wind carries no garden smell,
Should I believe I dreamed it
Any more than I dreamed the world,
The slums and mud flats,
The pear tree I once shook pears from?
Among the hours of hate, I can clear a space
For simple sorrow to breathe in.
When I find in a guard's face nothing I want to find,
I must imagine what he might have been,
The boy on the street on summer evenings
Playing hard at hide-and-go-seek,
Cheering as a friend scrambles across the lawn
To the home tree to free the prisoners.

IV

The world locks us away and forgets,
But we never forget the world.
And if you can come on diploma day,
You can watch the few men in the study program
Receive their scrolls in the visiting room,
Students of earth crust and epics,
Foreign policy, light refraction,
Roman history, the food chain.
You can see them in the honors block
Watching the evening news.

You'd be surprised how few laugh
When the President says that America
Will ignore the World Court for the next two years,
How many feel ashamed for him
As they walk back to their cells
To daydream in the hour before bed
That their crime is undone,
That a woman is lying on the cot with them
And the cot is a blanket under the stars.

Last month I sent you my thoughts on Jefferson.
This month I'm reading Russian thinkers.
I love the way they resist regret
And look ahead as Jefferson does
To a new order, with justice for all,
No masters and no slaves, no wars or colonies.
Were they studied today
By those with power in Moscow or Washington

More countries would be free now, and appeals
Wouldn't be piling up unread in the mailrooms.

No need for me to reread your words
To make me wonder what your life is like
And hope if you need help that help is coming,
Rumbling through the night by the truckload.
Meanwhile I can tell from here
How the letters in the Great Hall are hauled off
By the truckload to be burned,
How the smoke near the dump is so thick
The neighbors complain in letters to the authorities.

V

I'll be all right when I get out of here
If I don't look back to wonder who I might have been
Had I never been locked away
And don't live fast, trying to make the years up.

Even here I've done what I could with books
To climb above the wall and guard towers
And look out over the trees I can't touch
Down through house windows and screen doors.
I can almost see the people sitting down to eat:
The happy ones easy to believe in
And the sad ones no more comforted by their paintings
Than I am by my iron bed
Or my steel sink and toilet bowl.

And when the guards yell at me to come down,
I don't allow my anger to flare out
As I strain to catch the talk in the dining room.

And if the cries of the boy I was
Rise to my lookout, I don't look back on his beatings
And lament. I climb higher, so high
Even the sobs of the grown man for the boy
Can't reach me.

Like the sailors in the story
With wax stuffed in their ears, not like the hero,
I sail by, and my ship isn't turned toward home.
The future must contain what I haven't seen
In a place I've never visited
If it's holding something good in store for me.

FOR JOHN HEMMERS

Little League

It must be different in the other kingdom in June
When the Little Leaguers are out, screaming in the lots,
And Mr. Dellums, our old coach,
Doesn't have to settle in the outfield
For butterfingers like me or Harvey Schmitz,
For scatter-arms like Joe Dignam and Rubin Kornfeld,
But can choose his players among the best.
Not called on there to bench boys for catcalls
Or belabor the fundamentals till his voice goes raw.
He should be happy now if fielding an incredible team
Can make him happy. Why he wasted his time with us
Is a mystery. In love with the game, to be sure,
But not, surely, with the way we played it.
Four evenings a week and for no pay.
Maybe he wanted to show his gratitude
To old instructors who put up with his clumsiness.
But how will his heart be tested over there
Where nobody pushes his patience as we did
Past the breaking point? And how will he teach his team
Politeness toward teams with fewer advantages
If every team over there has new uniforms
And a coach to exemplify a plucky spirit,
No boys who must dream one up on their own?

Fear of the Dark

Fear of the dark stays with me but not the shame.
And the worry that my story won't reach the light
Where other stories wait and be understood
No longer seems a weakness I should overcome.

So what if it seems so to the few who require
Only themselves to fill their theaters. For them
It's a mystery why even Hamlet, no lover of the world,
Is anxious, dying, for the world to get the facts right

And makes Horatio promise to retell the play;
Why even the dead in Hell cry out to Dante
To carry their stories back; why Dante,
Banished from Florence, promises.

No need for anyone who doesn't ask to be heard
To hear the dead of Sodom crying for an audience
Though it's likely some good men died in that fire,
Fathers to widows and orphans, friends to the poor.

After the ashes settled, the scribes blackened the name
Of the charred walls to keep God's name pure.
It won't be easy to say enough
To get those ghosts to rest in the dark

As Troy rests, its ashes content with Homer's account
Of its long war and fiery fall,
Beautiful Troy, city beloved of Zeus,
Whose altars day and night smoked with offerings.

On the Soul

They told you you owned it and you believed them,
Flattered as if a real-estate man,
Pointing to a mansion with a lofty portico
On the crest of a hill, had assured you it was yours,
And the dream sounded too good to be resisted
Even when the doorman had sent you around back,
Even after ten years' work in the kitchen,
Ten years on your bed of straw
Dreaming of the empty suite upstairs
And of the empty bed with the crown
Hanging from the bedpost, bejeweled with your name.

It would have been better if they'd said nothing,
Or told you it lived its own life, like deer
Hidden in the woods, not seen from the road
As you drive past in the car, not seen
When you stop and climb the fence.
Even if they browse on your own land,
They're happiest left alone,
Stepping down in the evening to the stream,
Bedding down in silence under a screen of thickets
To dream what you may guess at and can't know.

At Becky's Piano Recital

She screws her face up as she nears the hard parts,
Then beams with relief as she makes it through,
Just as she did listening on the edge of her chair
To the children who played before her,
Wincing and smiling for them
As if she doesn't regard them as competitors
And is free of the need to be first
That vexes many all their lives.
I hope she stays like this,
Her windows open on all sides to a breeze
Pungent with sea spray or meadow pollen.
Maybe her patience this morning at the pond
Was another good sign,
The way she waited for the frog to croak again
So she could find its hiding place and admire it.
There it was, in the reeds, to any casual passerby
Only a fist-sized speckled stone.
All the way home she wondered out loud
What kind of enemies a frog must have
To make it live so hidden, so disguised.
Whatever enemies follow her when she's grown,
Whatever worry or anger drives her at night from her room
To walk in the gusty rain past the town edge,
Her spirit, after an hour, will do what it can
To be distracted by the light of a farmhouse.
What are they doing up there so late,
She'll wonder, then watch in her mind's eye
As the family huddles in the kitchen
To worry if the bank will be satisfied
This month with only half a payment,
If the letter from the wandering son
Really means he's coming home soon.

Even old age won't cramp her
If she loses herself on her evening walk
In piano music drifting from a house
And imagines the upright in the parlor
And the girl working up the same hard passages.

The Circus

If you've done things you should still feel sorry for,
Then sending your check to the Shriner's Circus Fund
For Crippled Children won't make you feel good

Any more than it's made the wife-beater feel good
Or the loan shark or the bookkeeper at the missile plant.
Send it simply, as they do, to sponsor a little joy.

Then if you sit in the crowd you'll wonder
If the crippled children should be laughing with the healthy ones
Or shaking their fists at the roof instead with Job's wife,

Resolved not to accept what they'd never have to
In a world carefully planned and made.
From your seat in back something will look so wrong

It will dawn on you why the maker was afraid
When Adam and Eve ate from the Tree of Knowledge,
Afraid they'd notice his slipshod craftsmanship.

It won't surprise you then that many aspire to leave,
That the ladder that Plato climbed led him away
From the visible kingdom to a beauty that didn't exist

And never would, that wasn't responsible
For the pitiful imitations. No wonder the couple
On the high trapeze delights the children so much,

Flouting the cloddish law of gravity, trying to be birds.
And then the army of clowns climbing out of the car
That by any law of matter couldn't hold four.

And still they come, another and another,
While those in the crowd who can't jump up
Strain forward in their seats to cheer them on.

On the Way to School

Even a lover of the bare truth must admit
This new façade painted on the high-rise
Is a big improvement over the blank face,
Pillars and capitals freshly applied
With a golden pediment and a frieze.
They seem to float above the bare bricks
Like a blurred dream, an admission
Of how much beauty the bricks left out.

Even art that remembers to build beauty in
Has to confine itself to a single theme and exclude
Most of the beautiful truths available,
Even the epic I like to teach each fall
Where the great battle is still raging,
Every hour more proof of how angry Achilles is.
His friends keep losing ground and he still won't help.

What Homer leaves out to concentrate on a war
He points to openly in the similes.
It relieves him to say the battle turns at the hour
When the woodcutter loads his wagon and heads home,
To compare soldiers crowding in for a kill
To summer flies clustering on a milking pail.

When Achilles yields to Priam
And unties the corpse of Hector from his chariot,
He seems to guess that something has been left out
In his quest for glory, as his quest for glory
Reminds me what I miss to rebuff the world.

This morning, on my way to school,
The sun, striking the high-rise head on,

Turns its painted face so shimmery
The illusion takes me in, marble as rich in detail
As the real marble of the city hall
Put up when the romance of commerce and self-rule
Was still strong, Syracuse and Arcade
In friendly competition with Troy and Ithaca,
Doric columns rising a hundred feet from the forest
For a city that didn't exist then and doesn't now.

No details are left out when Homer stops the fighting
For a thousand lines to describe the world
Crowding the face of Achilles' shield.
Here are the two cities in gold relief,
The wedding, the trial in the marketplace,
The harvest and the harvest festival.
Boys and girls dance on the polished dancing floor.
All this Achilles carries on his arm,
Which seems to mean he knows,
When he sees death coming, what life includes,
What exactly death leaves out.

from
Meetings with Time
(1992)

The Photograph

The background's blurred, so I can't be certain
If this showboat is docked on a river or a lake,
But the clothes of the dancers on deck
Make clear it's summer in the early forties,
And the long shadows suggest it's almost sundown.

No way to guess the song the couples are dancing to
But it looks like most are enjoying it.
The sadness that seems ingrained in the late light
Is the usual sadness of photographs, not theirs,
The feeling that comes from wondering
How few of the dancers welcome the light now.

And if I see them as ignorant, too confident in the future,
It's only because they're dancing in my childhood.
No reason to believe that the chubby man in the foreground
With his hand on the waist of the smiling blonde
Hasn't stepped back often to observe how his life
Is almost half gone and then returned
To press the moment more eagerly than before.

Here he is, back with the blonde girl,
Whose smile seems nervous now, who may be wondering,
When he's silent, if he's drifting off.
Did she say something she shouldn't have,
Or is he distracted by the man with the camera
Focusing by the taffrail?
Is he troubled to think of himself as old
Looking back on a photograph of this moment
When his heart was younger and more beautiful?

Don't worry about it, I want to tell them.
Don't waste your time with recollection or prophecy.
Step forward while the light and shadows are still clear,
The sun, low on the water, still steady.
Enter the moment you seem to be living in.

Defining Time

If it's like a river, the current is too much for us,
Sweeping us past a moment we're still not used to
Out to the void of the not-yet-come.
Should we resist, wherever we are,
Or be reconciled?
It seems to bring us gifts. Each day
Arrives as a fresh basket of bread.
Our right hand no longer can touch our left
Around the girth of our Buddha bellies.
How can that be if the minutes of the day are fish
Nibbling away at us till our bones show through,
Nibbling away at our friends, our houses?
Let's try to ignore it, whatever it is,
As we do the thin air of the Himalayas
When we climb, breathless, to pray for enlightenment.
Can we really ignore its earthly mass
As it lies between us and the thing we hope for?
A long wait till the train goes by
And we can cross the tracks into the evening,
Our favorite time. At last we're walking after dinner
On our ritual mile to the great magnolia.
There it is, glimmering at the end of the field.
Just a handful of whatever time is
And we'll be standing beneath its branches
Looking back at the poplars we're passing now.
How young we were back there, we'll say,
How confused and moody in that early era.
We need more time to consider it,
More than the dole allowed us at any moment,
The nickels and dimes.
We need to unfold time on the table like a map,
With the years gone and the years to come

Colored as vividly as the moment,
Proving how little it means to say
Time has gone by, passed through us
Or around us, and left us old.

My Guardians

Not aloof like the famous sky gods,
They keep just one lesson ahead of me,
As uncertain as I am about final things,
Stumped yesterday in Bible class
By the verses that now stump me.
They can't resolve the question
About heaven's kingdom,
How far it lies if it lies within.
They're only an hour or so in front
As they walk home after the concert,
Asking themselves what I'll be asking soon,
Where exactly the music's gone,
Whether the difference between what is and was
Is as vast as it seems and as final.
I'm walking their narrow trail across the country.
The embers of their fire are still warm
As I make my fire and snuggle in,
Happy, as I fall asleep, with the thought
That I'm keeping my true pace,
Not so slow that I lose them,
Not so quick that I pass them unawares.
When I'm lost, I know I've arrived
At the same spot where they were lost,
My wavering steps in the thicket
Proof of my loyalty, my tentative circles
Tramping their circles deep and clear.

Tuesday at First Presbyterian

Though he wheezes a little, and is stooped, and fat,
Our speaker this evening at First Presbyterian
Warms to his subject in the chilly church hall,
Not afraid to expose the greed of the big polluters
Or the sloth of the small. A man with a mission,
Who's willing to take the planet under his wing
As he might an orphan, who deserves a poem in a high style
That can lift a lowly subject like recycling,
The use of trash as raw material.
The odds against his success are longer by far
Than the odds in many stretches of hexameter.
Whatever Odysseus does to charm a king and queen
Famous for courtesy as they linger over wine,
Reclining on couches in the marble banquet hall,
Is nothing compared to reaching us few in the pews
As we sit here fretting over colds, delinquent bills,
Problem children we have to run back to.
Ten minutes of facing us is enough
To make our speaker drift to an island
Farther than a sea nymph's hideaway.
We can see him walking the beach collecting driftwood.
We can see him resting in the hut of a forester.
A note on the table points to jars of nuts and raisins
Cooling in the dark under the floorboards.
A map marks the secret path to the brook.
Just imagine the blessed few he wants to find there,
Kneeling by the clear pool, cupping their hands.
But now he's rowing back to our church
To resume his lecture on mortal rivers
Flowing through fragile drainage basins.
For his sake we should pay attention,

If we can't be moved directly by the water itself,
Slaking the thirst of us all, the just and unjust,
In smoky city streets and dusty farmlands.

The Window in Spring

These weed-grown car hulks rusting in my neighbor's yard
Could be read as tokens of disdain for my neatness
Or as mere indifference to my feelings
If he weren't civil in other ways,
If he didn't take in my papers
When I go on vacation and forget to cancel.

When the eyesore rankles, I tell myself
He could be cooling his flesh with gloomy reminders
Like a hermit contemplating a skull
After the fall of Rome, killing off his hunger
For any abiding place on earth.

On my side of the fence, my garden
Already green, my apple trees and Japanese plums
Proclaim the triumph of husbandry
Dear to the yeomen of the republic,
Disciples of Jefferson.

I was the confident boy in grade school
Shouting the Pledge of Allegiance,
A natural patriot.
He may have been the nervous boy in back
Mouthing the words he couldn't feel,
Destined from the first to be a stranger.

Could be there's a cold mother behind him
Or an absent father, whose father in turn
Lost all he had in the Great Crash.

It's a free country when two perspectives like ours
Live side by side without rancor.

No one strolling our block can complain of boredom
Or a lack of options. Door-to-door salesmen
Won't prosper here unless they can vary their pitch,
Masters of many strategies, not merely one.

They tend to choose my house,
The house of a man who clearly cares about upkeep,
Gutters and siding, while my neighbor's junkyard
Seems, in its want of pretension,
Attractive to Witnesses for Jehovah,
Who come Sundays in pairs,
Bibles in hand, to fish for souls.

One of them could have been the girl in my grade school
Whose parents thought the Pledge a form of idolatry,
Who sat, hands folded tight, in silence.
If my parents had raised her, she'd be at home now
Weeding her flower garden or watching the news.

But here she is, or someone like her,
Venturing up my walk as the Bible commands.
She's going to ask what truth I rely on
To save the world, and what's my plan exactly
For convincing my neighbor he isn't stranded in Sodom
With no escape car while the streets are burning.

Haven

It can't be Athens, this town
We don't inhabit but carry with us,
For here Socrates hasn't been tried and silenced.
Here he's still at his post on the curb,
Challenging any citizen who pretends
To be an expert on the good life.
And the young still gather to watch
As the proud man is discomfited.
But here, instead of vowing revenge,
As he might in Athens, the man feels grateful,
Eager to get home and report that fame
And power aren't as interesting as confusion.
"What a day!" he mutters to himself,
Pausing at the grocery
For a gift of pomegranates and plums.
We can't see his face as he waits in line,
But we know he's happy, just as happy
As the brother of the grocery man
Who lives over the store in one bare room,
A saint who just this moment
Has shown his passions the door
But not with the rancor common in other regions,
Not with the hate.
He wishes them well, a good home elsewhere.
And now, in the sudden quiet, he sits on his bed
And leafs through the town bible for inspiration.
Why not the chapter where Ahab forgives the whale
Or the one where Lear decides not to divide
His kingdom after all but to dine with Cordelia
In the main hall, off the best plates?
"What should we do," he asks, "with your sad sisters?"
Before she can answer, the saint jumps from his bed

And offers to walk the girls to the waterfront
And teach them how to hear the waves.
The sea that labors in other towns
Under a curse of silence seems here
To be waiting politely for the land to speak first.
And the land is clearing its throat to begin its solo
In a voice too gentle for us to catch
But not to praise.

Adventure

When we're tired of adventure, there's always Chekhov,
The challenge of a story like "A Journey by Cart,"
Where nothing happens that hasn't happened
Hundreds of times to the heroine,
A schoolteacher for thirty years.
She's made the monthly trip to the city in the provinces
And collected her salary, twenty rubles,
And now she's on her way back.
Twenty pages without incident
On a long day's bumpy journey by horse cart
To the ramshackle school, in the meager village,
Over a muddy road she knows too well.
Nothing happens to show her she's wrong
For wishing she could have lived instead in Moscow,
City of her childhood, and never become a teacher.
Need forced her, not faith in the calling.
And what faith could have lasted anyway
Out here, where schools are forgotten?

Are we supposed to notice something she's missing?
Is this a story where the heroine,
Preoccupied with her losses,
Fails to detect the delights available?
It's spring, after all. The snow has almost melted.
The woods smell piny and the air is clear.
Can spring be a substitute for a friend,
For someone who listens?
The landowner splashing by on his horse,
Handsome and smiling, slows down to chat,
But he isn't going to propose to her.
Their lives are too different, she sees,
And she's too old. He seems to like things

Just as they are, unmended.
He could have paved the swampy road
If he'd wanted to.

The cart bumps along again and nobody's different.
Even if we send her a hundred handbooks on charm
And she memorizes each one,
She'll remain where she is, in the cart with the driver,
Stubborn Semyon, who refuses to keep to the road,
Despite her urgings, in his quest for shortcuts.
And again the cart bogs down and fills with water.
Again the sugar and flour she's bought are ruined,
Her socks soaked and her feet numbed
By the time the roofs of the village edge into view.

"Don't plod on like this. Start over again
In a city with real choices," we'd call from our chairs
If we thought our voices could reach so far.
Now as she waits in the cart for a train to pass,
We want to believe she's resigned and hardened.
Too bad she glimpses in a flashing window a face
With her mother's high forehead and glossy hair.
That's all it takes for Moscow to flood back,
The easy talk in the bright parlor,
The piano and the goldfish bowl,
The girl she was, still young and gaily dressed,
Awakened from a dream of thirty years.

And then the vision's gone and the train.
And here's the village. The story's over.
Do we leave her there?
Do we let her go in alone

To light the stove in her frosty bedroom,
Our sister, who's growing old with us,
Whose crossroads are all behind her?
We have to get back to Moscow,
To our family, to our friends who miss us.

From the window of the train we glimpse her
Huddled in the cart back at the crossing.
Any words of advice we think of shouting
She's thought of long ago on her own.
Just time enough for a nod and a wave.
Then we sit back with the wish
She could read the story we've read
And see her life carried over into art,
Generous art where she's the heroine.

The Bill of Rights

You're free to imagine many lives
Though only one's allowed your body,
The body you didn't choose,
Small-boned and thin like Grampa Wheelock's.
Among the songs your elders sang
You were free to pick the one you preferred
And sing it with your own inflections
To the baby sister you were asked to watch.
It was your decision to save half your summer pay
For the teachers college your uncle went to,
To see its closeness as an advantage.
You were free to walk home on the route you fancied
From Ferguson Elementary to the woman you chose,
The sweetheart with your sister's long hair
And the dark eyes of Miss Gorse,
Your Latin teacher in high school,
Who told you you'd go far
If you learned to trust your feelings.
Nobody forced you to buy a house
Near the sycamore trees you climbed as a boy.
Its features pleased you most
Just as you're pleased this sunny Sunday
To climb the ladder and clean the roof drains,
Scooping out mud and sycamore leaves.
And now you choose to pause in your work
And look out over the valley town.
There's the Dalys' slate roof
And the Hendersons' shingles.
There's the smokestack of the bottle plant
And the blue patch of the water tower.
This must be one of the vistas held out to you
Before you were born, one of the many

You were free to choose from.
And now you're free to guess what spirit
Guided your pointing hand that day.
You're free to wonder who whispered in your ear
As clearly as your daughters are calling now,
"Come down, Dad. Come down."
They want to show you the flowers they found
Streaked like the ones you picked for them last fall
Behind the school you sent them to.

The Invalid

Today they'd have found a way to get me and my chair
Up the thirty steps of the high school, but then
It seemed impossible, as if the ramp had yet to be invented,
As if two strong boys couldn't carry a skinny girl.
Hearts weren't smaller back then; my friends were loyal.
They visited me at home just as you do now.
But imagination was more confined.
Even my parents couldn't think of a way around it.
And I too learned to see it as a fate
I was foolish to complain against.
Of course I managed to learn at home
As much or more than my friends at school,
Scored higher on achievement tests,
Grew more curious about the world.
Still it seemed I was waving from the dock
While they sailed away to the future.
Now I know that metaphor was mistaken.
I too have traveled in spirit, though given the choice
To live again as I did or with one amendment
I'd choose to try my chances without the polio.
Wisdom isn't the only thing worth having.
Wiser or not, I'd have felt more free.
Free or not, I'd be richer now in memories,
No small matter for an old woman like me
Sitting in a sunny yard under a plum tree,
A blanket on my wasted legs in mid-July.
Not that I don't take comfort from what I've done,
The way I resisted anger and envy
And worked to make my fretful disposition serene,
The wishes that lead to disappointment abandoned,
Worked to live in the moment like this plum tree.
Whatever it's planned to do it's doing now

Between the garage that needs to be torn down
And the fence that needs repairing.
I've tried to be like a character in a play
Who is nothing but what she says and does,
With nothing held in to fester between scenes
While the crowd goes out to the lobby for a smoke.
What about dinner, they ask, at Roma's or André's?
What about starting over in Fresno or Spokane
Where people are rumored to be more sensitive
To genius of the subtler kind?
I hope it isn't merely ignorance of its death
That makes this tree look tranquil,
Or its saintly diet of air and water,
Which has always been too pure for me.

The Anthropic Cosmological Principle

Maybe the new theory is true, and the odds
For intelligent life beyond our planet
Are even slimmer than they were here,
And the only voices ever to reach us
From beyond will be our children's,
Our earth in a thousand years the mother of colonies
On planets never before inhabited.

Long after the sun swells in its final flare
To consume our world, they'll remember us
Just as immigrants here remember the old country in stories.
The Earth will sound to them like a garden,
More a land of myth than of history,
Its green valleys and blue skies incredible,
The way its grasses climbed the hills untended,
The way its birds alighted in groves nobody planted
To trill phrases nobody taught them.

A house like this one, on a street like mine,
Will be a house from a dim, heroic age
When their own fate was decided. Just as I stay up late
To study a narrative of the Civil War
And marvel how close the country came to dissolving,
The great experiment cancelled, the slaves still slaves,
So they will marvel as they study our hostilities
How close we came to spoiling their chances,
Their galactic cities bombed into fictions, their farms,
Schools, churches, opera houses, and union halls
Sponged from the blackboard with the crowds
Down on the dock for Regatta Day.

Are they real or not? That's the question
That has them worried. Are they waiting on a road
Reachable from the starting point of today?
Impossible to imagine how remote I'd feel
After rummaging in a trunk all afternoon,
Searching for proof that I paid my taxes,
If I found a letter proving I was never born,
That the mother who might have been mine
Ran off on her wedding day and was never heard from,
That I'm only my would-be father's fantasy
As he lies in his empty house on his deathbed
Dreaming of the life he might have lived.

Today I seem to be real as I stop for groceries.
I may be moody returning to the empty house
I promised myself to fill, but not so lonely
If I think of the distant, stellar observers.
What voices deeper than reason and will
I've failed to hear isn't so hard a question
As why I've been fated to decide their destiny.
And what's my strategy for the day, they wonder,
To prompt them to practice songs of joy,
Not dirges?

Unfinished Symphony

Not far from here, as we stroll to the square at sundown,
An old man, writing in his room,
Resists the wind-borne noises of traffic and street games,
The click of heels in the cobbled alley.
He's nearing the end of his great project.
He's almost ready to prove that couples like us
Are strolling to the only square available
In the only world we could be strolling in.
However chosen the moment seems to us,
From where he sits it's always waited
Patiently in the half-light for us to arrive
Over the only road we could have come.
And even when we turned down side roads
To explore the villages, we were still approaching,
Even while unfolding a blanket in the meadow
Beside a stream, sharing a taste of the local wine,
Napping beside the willows.
That's what his love for the truth
Seems to be pushing him to prove once and for all
Though now a breeze from the world of might-have-been
Reaches his window, and he smells the grass himself
And pauses a moment in his argument.
The hardest part's to come, the part where he shows
How the continent had to be settled as it was,
How the Indians had to be waiting for the Conquistadors,
How their ancestors, eons before,
Had to wander across from Asia on the land bridge,
Dancing their Tartar dances, singing their songs.
Down the coast they ventured and inland,
Wrapped in blankets their dark-haired women wove,
Dark hair in long braids that swayed
As they walked in silence behind the dray.

Outside the window, a car door slams.
The old man steadies himself to go on
And show how necessary it was for them to vanish
With their deerskin dresses, their brooches of bone.
He'll finish soon if he doesn't imagine them
Pausing on their trek a few yards from his house
To camp for the night. No going on without them
If the women start combing their hair out
Or sing to the sun their songs of sundown
As they always do.

Mildew

Till now a subject mentioned only as a metaphor
To stand for mustiness in the soul.
But here we have the genuine article
Growing on the north wall of my neighbor's house
That's cost him too much already in upkeep.
Black streaks over blue paint that was guaranteed
Against fungus of all kinds, returning each fall
After its spring treatment of bleach.
He scrubbed the bottom story himself
And would have done the rest if the gutter
He'd tried to unclog last fall
Hadn't pulled loose, spooking him about ladders.
Black streaks and a musty smell in the guest room
That stumps the experts. Long before now
He guessed he was only a transient on the planet.
Now it's clear his house is a transient too,
Though this evening its lights are burning warmly.
In a minute his Thanksgiving guests will arrive
Having outdone themselves with their walnut stuffing,
Having added new stories to their portfolios.
Their cheerful, spirited talk will fill the kitchen.
He won't interrupt to ask if they can explain
Why his is the only house on the block
With a mildew problem. Bad luck, maybe,
Though in an earlier era it would be a warning
To turn from a world he's loved too much.
But what other world steps forward now
To offer its services? And even if it did,
What deserves more of his gratitude
Than his clapboard guardian against wind and rain,
A basement haven for Ping-Pong on winter evenings,
An attic skylight for reattaching to stars

The names washed off by the daily drizzle?
Mildew creeps to the house unseen and suddenly
Scales the walls. But not for him anymore
The temptation of the underground passage
Past the enemy line to a hidden harbor
Where he can still imagine a rowboat waiting.

Night Walk

At midnight, when you hit a snag in your essay
Describing the light only a few can love,
The few who are most awake, do what I do.
Stroll on Main Street past the lighted storefronts.
Pause to peer in the window of Spiegel's Appliances
Past the dishwashers and floor fans.

You should recognize the watchman slumped in his chair.
It's our butcher, yours and mine,
Moonlighting here as he's done for years
Ever since Brenda asked him for a sailboat
Like the one in the cigarette ad,
Complete with cabin, deck chair, and flag.

After you've pitied him for a while, as I have,
How he's mortgaged himself to tinsel,
Boats and beauties, while the time grows late
And the first page in the book of life
Is still not filled, notice how peaceful his sleep seems,
The sleep of a man happy to drowse through weekdays
So he can snap awake on the weekend
To Brenda dangling her long legs from the bow
Or lying back in her chair, eyes closed.
Why climb the lookout if he has all he's ever wanted?
Why not crawl back and forth on his knees,
Scrubbing the deck down while she dozes,
Or polish the chrome, already rusting?

And after you've asked yourself, as I have, if her smile
Can really last him all week in the undergloom
Of meats and motors, assuming she's smiling at him,
Not merely at the wind for stroking her face,

Ask when the truth you've followed has once smiled back,
Once dropped a note on your plate praising your loyalty.
"Brenda," his tombstone will say,
If the carver wants to record the love of his life.
And what about yours? What word
Would you like lovers and loners to read
As they stroll on Sundays the shady, municipal graveyard,
What truth you loved in your few moments of clarity?

Infidel

If I chew these sesame seeds slowly,
As the book advises, and do my rhythmic breathing,
I may end the year as a journeyman to Buddha,
Soon to join the circle of his companions.

No more wasting my energy on my will,
The will that butts its way through the crowd,
Shoulders stooped under its sack of ambitions.
I can walk behind it at a saving distance,
Glancing about me, not straight ahead.

Soon, if I chew these sesame seeds slowly,
I'll wonder what it's like to be a stone,
Or a tree, or the dog asleep by the lawn chair,
Or the woman in the chair, gray-haired and frail,
Knitting a sweater for her daughter's baby.

To be them, and then to leave them.
To hope they're not as stranded in what they are
As the blue flowers in the yard at the corner
Which seem to keep shouting only one name,
Blue flower, blue flower.

Just a mouthful of sesame seeds and salt
To neutralize the acidity of the blood
And maybe in a week or two the fretful yin child
Will be a contemplative, joyful yang.

And if I can change, my friends can follow
If they're willing to be more flexible

And don't insist, as they have till now,
On their own vivid, unchastened perspectives.

Strange to love those who resist me,
Who block the sidewalk when I go exploring
And won't give ground, who force me
To step aside with my ears ringing,
My eyes watering, and move on

Under awnings that flap their colors
As awnings do, under lindens
Shaking their leaves as lindens will
When they want to refresh themselves
In gusts blowing now from the mountains,
Now from the sea.

My Moses

Time to praise the other Moses, the one who concludes
That the bush isn't really burning, as he first supposed,
Just backlit in red by the setting sun,
Magnified by the need of a runaway to be pardoned,
To pull his shoes off and receive a vision.
The Moses who, when he lifts his staff,
Can't part the waters, who has to wade in
At low tide and hope for the best.
Nobody drowns. Nobody's following. The twelve tribes,
Sluggish after a hard day in the quarries,
Didn't find his lecture on the virtues inspiring.
And Pharaoh was willing to see him go.
Good riddance, what with his praise of creation
That gouged the work month with holidays.
Now he's wringing his clothes out on the other side,
Relieved it hasn't taken him any longer to realize
He isn't much of a prophet, that he hasn't the gift.
Free now of the journey to the Promised Land
And the wars with the natives, he can settle down at once
Whenever he pleases, and be happy even here
In the country that disappointed Columbus,
That wasn't the hoped-for shortcut to spices.
Happy even on this block of mine, my neighbor,
A civics teacher at the high school,
Who leaves the gate to his yard unlocked
So the neighborhood children can pick the berries
Before the frost comes and leaf smoke rises
From small, mute fires he's lit himself.

Delaware Park, 1990

These five students from China,
Cooking their dinner on the grill by the swings,
May be trying to resist the great temptation
Of feeling orphaned, reminding themselves instead
How they were lonely often back home too
And were happy to be neglected by the authorities.

This country, they could be saying,
May have felt just as alien
To the settlers who arrived early from Europe,
The odd ones who sold their old-country farms
For a passage to a land that for all they knew
Was merely hearsay. As for the Indians,
Who knows what homeland meant to them
When they woke to a vista of hills
Unmarked by clearings, barns, and orchards?

This park could be the one
Their children will play in
As if the benches were made for them,
As if they owned the sun and the clouds,
As if a rain like the one beginning to fall now
Disappointed them only as a friend would,
For reasons they could accept without knowing.

This day, they could be saying
As they gather their blankets, doesn't prove
The life here cold and unwelcoming.
The man who's watched them an hour from his bench
One day won't be a mystery.
They'll be able to guess what he's thinking

Just as they might guess a stranger's thoughts in China.
Today he seems knowing, confident, and remote.
One day he may seem confused and frail,
In need of sponsors. And they'll step forward
With solace they can't offer now.

Spring Letter

With the warmer days the shops on Elmwood
Stay open later, still busy long after sundown.
It looks like the neighborhood's coming back.
Gone are the boarded storefronts that you interpreted,
When you lived here, as an emblem of your private recession,
Your ship of state becalmed in the doldrums,
Your guiding stars obscured by fog. Now the cut-rate drugstore
Where you stocked your arsenal against migraine
Is an Asian emporium. Aisles of onyx, silk, and brass,
Of reed baskets so carefully woven and so inexpensive
Every house could have one, one work of art,
Though doubtless you'd refuse, brooding instead
On the weavers, their low wages and long hours,
The fruit of their labor stolen by middlemen.
Tomorrow I too may worry like that, but for now
I'm focusing on a mood of calm, a spirit of acceptance,
Loyal to my plan to keep my moods distinct
And do each justice, one by one.
The people in line for ice cream at the Sweet Tooth
Could be my aunts and uncles, nieces and nephews.
What ritual is more ancient or more peaceable?
Here are the old ones rewarding themselves
For making it to old age. Here are the children
Stunned into silence by the ten-foot list of flavors
From Mud Pie to Milky Way, a cosmic plenty.
And those neither young nor old, should they be loyal
To their favorite flavor or risk a new one?
It's a balmy night in western New York, in May,
Under the lights of Elmwood, which are too bright
For the stars to be visible as they pour down on my head
Their endless starry virtues. Nothing confines me.
Why you felt our town closing in, why here

You could never become whoever you wished to be,
Isn't easy to understand, but I'm trying.
Tomorrow I may ask myself again if my staying
Is a sign of greater enlightenment or smaller ambition.
But this evening, pausing by the window of Elmwood Liquors,
I want to applaud the prize-winning upstate Vouvray,
The equal of its kind in Europe, the sign says.
No time for a glass on your search
As you steer under stars too far to be friendly
Toward the island where True Beauty, the Princess,
Languishes as a prisoner. I can see you at the tiller
Squinting through spume, hoping your charts are accurate,
Hoping she can guess you're on your way.

Invitation

This is your invitation to the Ninth-Grade Play
At Jackson Park Middle School
8:00 P.M., November 17, 1947.
Macbeth, authored by Shakespeare
And directed by Mr. Grossman and Mrs. Silvio
With scenery from Miss Ferguson's art class.

A lot of effort has gone into it.
Dozens of students have chosen to stay after school
Week after week with their teachers
Just to prepare for this one evening,
A gift to lift you a moment beyond the usual.
Even if you've moved away, you'll want to return.
Jackson Park, in case you've forgotten, stands
At the end of Jackson Street at the top of the hill.

Doubtless you recall that *Macbeth* is about ambition.
This is the play for you if you've been tempted
To claw your way to the top. If you haven't been,
It should make you feel grateful.
Just allow time to get lost before arriving.
So many roads are ready to take you forward
Into the empty world to come, misty with promises.
So few will lead you back to what you've missed.

Just get an early start.
Call in sick to the office this once.
Postpone your vacation a day or two.
Prepare to find the road neglected,
The street signs rusted, the school dark,
The doors locked, the windows broken.
This is where the challenge comes in.

Do you suppose our country would have been settled
If the pioneers had worried about being lonely?

Somewhere the students are speaking the lines
You can't remember. Somewhere, days before that,
This invitation went out, this one you're reading
On your knees in the attic, the contents of a trunk
Piled beside you. Forget about your passport.
You don't need to go to Paris just yet.
Europe will seem even more beautiful
Once you complete the journey you begin today.

No Shame

No shame if you choose in the end
To be buried like an ancient Roman,
At the roadside,
The stone above you crowded with inscription,
Calling the passersby to pause
And read how you served the state,
How the scales of your butcher shop always read true,
How you cared for your small plot, a pious farmer.

No shame to hope for some visitors
Though maybe in life you grew accustomed to solitude,
Content to defend the good
As you spoke in the courtroom
Over the heads of the crowd
To the gods you imagined, who loved perfection.

Having proved you could live alone,
You can reach out in death to others
As the Romans did, with a few true phrases,
Learned early or late.
You who pass by, don't rely on doctors.
They're the ones who brought me here.
Reader of stones, if you're rich
Don't live meanly, as I did,
And stint on feast days.
Travelers, if you're poor, master one skill
So in one thing you can feel superior
And accept without shame,
When the time comes, the help of others.

Lying under your stone,
A coin of the realm over each eye,

The fee for Charon's ferry still unspent,
You'll pause in the endless review of memory
And the endless dream of returning
With a disposition that's more agreeable
And listen to the traffic of carts and chariots,
Mule shoes and horseshoes, sandals and clogs.

The few who pause above you
Will be just the ones most open to suggestions.
Their prayers haven't been answered.
Their best schemes have failed them.
Now they bend to read your conclusions.
No shame to teach in a roadside school
Students willing to learn from anyone.

from
Ranking the Wishes
(1997)

Loss

Just because your cousins perjured themselves
On the stand to steal the house you inherited
And have settled in, and are filling the rooms
With furniture your aunt would have hated,
Doesn't mean they're getting away with it.

Just because their lights will now burn late
In the house you love, and the sound of their dancing
Will be heard in the street, their drums and trumpets
At birthday parties, graduations, and weddings,
Doesn't mean they're not paying the penalty,
Living lesser lives than they might have lived,
Possessing lesser amounts of comeliness.

And if they're not aware of the loss,
Couldn't that show how shrunken their spirits are,
How you wouldn't want to be them as they fall asleep
At the end of a day they regard as perfect?

Of course it's hard not to wish them ill,
A pain that even their thicker souls can feel.
But that won't widen your cramped apartment.
That won't give you the spacious, airy life you admire
With windows opening out on the horizon.

Pity them if you can't forget them.
And if that's too hard for now, pity the house.
Think how it's losing out on the care
You'd have bestowed on it, on the loyalty
You'd have shown to its style and character,

Not to your fancy, a distinction too fine
For the new owners to handle.

Be like those angels said to enjoy the earth
As a summer retreat before man entered the picture,
Staggering under his sack of boundary stones.
They didn't mutter curses as they fastened their wings
And rose in widening farewell circles.
They grieved for the garden growing smaller below them,
Soon to exist only as a story
That every day grows harder to believe.

Pendulum

If I sleep through the moment just before dawn
When the pendulum of the day reaches the top
Of its swing and pauses, I can catch the other pause
At dusk, when the street outside the window
Appears suspended, lifted from its surroundings
And held motionless, and I'm able to ask
Why these particular houses have been selected
To compose my world, and why now,
When my soul feels fluid,
Kin to everyone who has ever lived here
From the time of the earliest settler till today.
A puff of wind in the snowball bush at the curb.
A puff over the waist-high, shaggy grass
Rolling away from the farmhouse in all directions
As a woman steps out on the porch in dusky light
To ring the bell. Just as she reaches up
To summon her son and husband from the barn
The pendulum of the day reaches its pausing point
And her gaze grows tentative and confused.
What is this place to her, this endless prairie,
This wilderness fit for a soul that asks to be lonely
Under a boundless sky, which she never asked for
Or only in one of her many moods.
Hasn't she dreamed for two nights running
Of a woman walking home from the opera
Through the streets of Paris, humming a theme?
Two women playing their parts in separate dramas
Or one woman divided. That's the issue for her
As she watches the grass from the porch
Billow and bend while time's suspended.
The wind crosses the prairie, skirts the woods,
And shakes the snowball bush at the curb

Across from the self-same row of houses,
Motionless and unyielding, blocking my vista.
And then her hand tightens on the rope
And the pendulum, poised, starts on its downswing
As the bell sounds, and the day parts
Soundlessly like the grass to let us in.

Days of Heaven

That was a great compliment the Greeks paid to human life
When they imagined their gods living as humans do,
With the same pleasure in love and feasting,
Headstrong as we are, turbulent, quick to anger,
Slow to forgive. Just like us, only immortal.
And now that those gods have proven mortal too
And heaven and earth can't be divided,
Every death means a divine occasion
Has been taken from us, a divine perspective,
Though the loss gets only a line or two in the news.
Hard to believe the headlines this morning
That a banker on Mt. Olympus has been pilfering,
That a builder has been guilty of shoddy construction
On a bridge that spans a river in heaven,
Cutting corners to squirrel away his fortune
For a better day, when the great day has already come.
For news that heartens we must turn to the classifieds.
Here in what's left of heaven it's right to advertise
For a soul mate. It's right to look for a job
That lets us incarnate spirit more fully
And leave something behind that time is kinder to
Than the flesh of gods. Lucky there's work.
Lucky the streets of heaven are in need of repair.
Paint is peeling from the dream-house trim.
Holy rainwater backs up in leaf-clogged gutters
Till the ceiling sags and tiles need regrouting.
And look at the list of practical items for sale—
Used snowblowers, croquet sets, chainlink fencing.
And what about a wooden canoe with two paddles.
Why don't we make time for a turn before sundown?
Out on the broad lake a breeze will find us
That's wafted around the planet to cool our divinity.

The clouds will hover above us in a giant halo
As we watch our brother, the sun, descend,
His gentle face turned toward us, his godly expression
Undarkened by accusation or disappointment
Or the thought of something he's left undone.

To Reason

I hope I never speak ill of you,
Dependable homely friend who prods me gently
To turn to the hour that's now arriving,
Not to the hour I let slip by
Twenty years back. No way now, you say,
To welcome a friend I failed to welcome
When she returned to town in sorrow,
Fresh from her discovery that the man
Who seemed to outshine all the others
Could also cast the densest shade.

You're right to label it magical thinking
When I say to a phantom what I never said
To flesh and blood, as if the words, repeated enough,
Could somehow work their way back to an old page
And nudge the silence aside and settle in, a delusion
Not appropriate for a man no longer young
At the end of a century where many nations
Have set many things in motion they can't call back
Though the vote for reversal is unanimous.

I'm glad you ask, clear-sighted Reason,
Before what audience, if my speech can't reach her ears,
I imagine myself performing. Who is it
I want to convince I'd do things differently
This time around if the chance were offered.
You're right to say that half an hour a day is enough
For these gods or angels to get the point
If they're ever gong to get it, which is doubtful.
Right again that if part of myself
After all my efforts still needs convincing

I should leave that dullard behind
With the empty dream of wholeness and move on.

I should move along the road that is not the road
I'd be moving along had I said what I didn't say
To someone who might have been ready to listen,
But a road as good, you assure me, Reason,
One that might lead to a life I can be proud of
So the man I might have been can't pity me.

Thanks for contending I can solve the problems
He may have wanted to solve but hadn't the time for,
Preoccupied as he was with another life,
The one I too might be caught up in
Had I heard the words you now speak clearly
Just as clearly long ago.

Cedar Point

The woman who cooked her heart out at Cedar Point
High in the Adirondacks wouldn't have minded so much
When nobody came to the kitchen to praise her work
If she'd believed her work recorded by a watchful heaven.
Sad that a faith like that was denied her,
That she lived in a skeptical, fretful era
Not rich in serious witnesses. The guests at Cedar Point,
Lacking either the taste required or the concentration,
Bolted dessert in their rush to get back to the lake
For an evening sail or ramble or bingo game.
In an age of faith the joy of achievement
Would have been enough, and she needn't have dreamed
Of consuming in vengeance a feast intended for fifty
All by herself while the guests ate crackers.
Just herself at the table with her one friend, Cindy,
The young, willowy waitress who never smiled,
Who was bullied all day by the manager
With his no-nonsense lantern jaw and raspy voice.
In an age of faith Cindy might have believed
Her sorrow recorded in a heavenly ledger,
But in the age she lived in only the helpless cook
Looked on with concern and maybe the gentle boy
At table seven, who asked her questions.
As for the faith of the boy, he could imagine a potion
That Cindy's stepmother, desperate for youth,
Received for abandoning Cindy to the manager,
But not a potion to make a boy of eleven
A knight by summer's end, a deliverer.
And now, forty years later, when the cook
Has long since sweated her last in the thankless kitchen,
The whole burden of witnessing falls on him.
Even the woman that Cindy's become

Might not remember, sixty years old at least
If still alive, retired to Florida for all he knows,
Carting her grandchildren to baseball practice
While her husband, sporty in cleats and cap,
Tees off with his chums. No witness left
But a man who admits he has no answers
As he asks how to save Cindy the Beautiful
Still stranded in her attic room,
Ironing the uniform of her prison
Or lugging the heavy trays
From the steamy kitchen without a smile,
Not expecting her luck to change.

The Great Day

What if the great day never comes
And your life doesn't shine with vivid blossoms,
Just with the usual pale variety?
What if the best china never seems called for,
Those dishes reserved for the friends you love the most
On the day they return from their endless travels?
To use them now, for the only occasions available,
Would be to confuse the high realm with the low.
But not to use them, doesn't that seem wrong too,
To leave the best wine undrunk in the cellar
For the next owner of your house to open?
What then? Can you will yourself to see a common day
The way a saint might see it, as a gift from heaven,
Or the way it appears from the window of the hospital
On the first morning the patient feels strong enough
To edge across the room and look out?
There on the street an angel policeman
Is directing the flashing mosaic of traffic.
Or can you see the day as the dead might see it,
Not the ones who'd rather rest but those delighted
To abandon the gardens of Hell, however fragrant,
For a chance at crossing the sea again in a storm?
The day their ship, long given up for lost,
Steams into the harbor, all flags flying,
Would be a day to be toasted with rose champagne
In heirloom glasses. Down the gangway they come,
A little thinner, a little unsteady,
Eyes wide in wonder at their rare good fortune.
Can you see what they see as they look around
Or feel what their friends waiting on the dock

Must feel as they run forward?
"Let me look at you," they keep saying,
Suspending their formal speech of welcome.
"You look good. You look wonderful."

Seven Days

No problem making sense of the week
Once I convince myself that each day
Is meant to follow the one before
Or not to follow, whichever it chooses.
One day for me to be the rabbi upstairs
Mapping the twelve degrees of righteousness.
One day to put the first degree into practice,
Figuring how to allow the gleaners
To gather sheaves in my field after the harvest
When I have no field, just a yard in town.
And then a sunny day for making my yard
A kingdom of flowers to delight the eye.
And a rainy day for sketching the yellow flower
Adorning the hair of the goddess Luna
As she rows her boat through a black sky.
And then a day to be sad this image of fulfillment
Would be just as strange to the rabbi
As his love of commandments would be to her,
However many letters I carried between them.
And a day to be happy I can talk to one
And then the other, and agree with both,
Undaunted by contradiction and inconsistency.
And then one day of rest from wondering
If I'm to bless them as my own creation
Or if they're to bless me as their restless child.

Sarit Narai

Now that the light holds on after supper,
Why not walk west to the end of Ferry Street
And linger where the ferries used to dock
Before the bridge spanned the Niagara.
Why not enlarge the thin verge of the moment
With the Sunday crowd on deck fifty years ago
Riding to Fort Erie and back just for the fun of it.
The wind from the lake ruffles their hair
As the low sun glances along the water.
Just as they left their rooms to join the flow
So you can go back to them for a moment
And lead them forward into the present
Where the gulls are gliding, swinging beneath the bridge
In figures that blur as you watch, and disappear.
And why not call up the boys you used to see here
Playing on the boulders in the bridge's shadow
Before the fence was put up to stop them.
If one of them lost his footing, his chances were slim,
The push in the channel too hard and heavy,
The water of Erie beginning its headlong, brainless rush
To join the Ontario, as if an extra minute mattered.
Remember the evening you found a crowd here
Waiting beside an ambulance with its motor running
And a squad car where a woman sat in back
Head in her hands? Dark-haired. Next morning
Leafing through the local news, you found the story—
Woman from Thailand, three years in the States,
Loses her son, eleven, to the Niagara.
Let yourself go, if you want to enlarge the moment,
And imagine what might have happened if the boy,
Sarit Narai, had been fished from the river in time.
Try to think of him as your son's best friend

At Niagara school, where friends were scarce,
Quieting a wildness you could never manage,
The mild manners of Asia persuasive by mere example.
And what if your daughter admires him even more
And comes to choose him for her life's companion,
Not the drab complainer she ended up with.
The world turned left that day on the forking path
But the path on the right still runs beside it
Though never touching. A bountiful Buddha smile
As he explains to your granddaughters and grandsons
How to climb the eightfold path to freedom
As gulls like these swoop over the gray stones
And the ferries steam back and forth if you let them.
Freely the crowd on deck empties its mind of thought
And welcomes sensation, the sun and wind.
And then the riders waken to see the skyline of home
Beckoning from a distance as if it missed them,
So they're ready to take up their lives again
As the ship pulls in where now a line of cars
Waits in the twilight to pay the bridge toll
Not thirty yards from the spot where the ambulance waited
And the woman cried in the back seat of the car.
After an hour the crowd moved off, dissolving to families,
To couples musing on twilight pastimes.
For a moment, though, each may have hesitated
To change the subject and appear small-souled,
The mist of sorrow already thinning and fading
That would have remained if they'd lived in Eden,
The one kingdom where the sorrows of others
Feel like our own. When Buddha neared Nirvana,
One story goes, he looked back on us as we drowned
In the sea of endless craving, and was filled with pity,

And chose to postpone his bliss till all were saved.
But how can a climb from the world be managed here
When the crowd on the ferry wants the sunset to linger,
And the mother would sell her soul to get her son back,
And the boy still struggles to grab the slippery rock
And pull himself up, his friends all helping
So he can grow old among them. An old man
Looking back on his deeds of kindness. Now the few
Who met him and the many who never did but might have
Feel the phantom gap he would have filled
But are ignorant of its cause and blame their wives,
Their husbands, their children, their towns and jobs,
And hunt around for new gospels, new philosophies.
If you see them this evening pacing along the bank
Where once the ferries docked and the Sunday riders
Lost themselves awhile in the sway and shimmer,
Pity their restlessness. There must be a way
To step forward and name the one they miss,
Sarit Narai, in a tone so resonant
It holds them a moment beyond loss and longing.

Aunt Celia, 1961

A life without remorse, that's something
I'm willing to predict for a generous,
Brave young man like you. But as for happiness,
There you need luck, the kind I had
In meeting your Uncle Harry after I'd given up
Thinking I'd find a man to suit me.
The blind luck of visiting a cousin in Pittsburgh
In the spring of 1930, of going along
When she went to the lecture at the socialist club,
Of sitting at the back of the hall near the exit,
Of forgetting my scarf and having to run back,
Of stumbling over a chair and falling.
A fretful, impulsive girl helped to her feet by a man
Who turned out cheerful and philosophical.

It isn't gratitude that I felt then or feel now.
More a mixture of wonder, relief, and fear
When I imagine the girl I was back then
Making do with the luck most people have,
Missing the unknown rendezvous by inches,
The scarf not left behind, the meeting canceled,
The trip to Pittsburgh postponed a week
So she could be home for her mother's birthday.

People will tell you there are many good lives
Waiting for everyone, each fine in its own way.
And maybe they're right, but in my opinion
One is miles above the others.
Otherwise it wouldn't have been so clear to me
When I found it. Otherwise those who lack it
Wouldn't be able to tell so clearly it's missing
As they go on living as best they can

Without complaining. Noble lives, and beautiful,
And happy as much as doing well can make them.
But as for the happiness that can't be earned,
The kind it makes no sense for you to look for,
That's something different.

All I've Wanted

Who's to say that Mrs. Gottlieb, a woman of spirit,
Wasn't right when she told our high-school class
People get what they really want,
Right in her case, at least, and in mine.
I might have learned Greek if I'd wanted to.
The dictionary and grammar book on my shelf
Were likely symbols of a wish not deep enough
To issue in practice. I might have gone to Bali
And witnessed the fire dance that my friend described
So vividly I bought a map of the island,
Brochures on accommodations, a silk shirt for the climate.
I probably thought I'd be happier here
Doing other things, some less taxing than travel,
Some more. Could be I didn't want my second choice
For heart's companion deeply enough to make her stay.
Could be I wanted the seven years of regret that followed.
It's likely I could have explored whatever it was
That blocked the flow of feeling from heart
To tongue if I'd made the effort,
Could have dug the silt from the living stream.
I must have had other projects in mind,
Other ideas for ranking the needs of my species
According to a personal formula I can't call up now
But doubtless could if I wanted to.
I must want to keep that question open
Like the question whether I'm the laborer
Who reports for work in the vineyard at the crack of dawn
Or the one who straggles in at dusk with no excuses,
Hoping this is the place where the last are first.
I must enjoy not knowing if my walk this evening
Marked the end of a full day or a day of waiting.
I must be glad that the flock of plover

Arcing above the school in close formation
Looked set apart in their own blue world,
Not heading for any retreat we share.

Integer

Shall I give up on salvation
And suppose the unit of life isn't the self,
As I've always assumed, but the twenty houses
That make up my block? Which house puts in the hours
Required each month by the block's one conscience
Won't be the issue then, as long as the slot gets filled.
A comfort then to wake before dawn
And glimpse through curtains the light
Already burning in my neighbor's study,
Proof that the block's quota of early writing
Is on its way to completion and I can sleep in
Or drive to the farmer's market for groceries
Since shopping too is a category of useful action
And spaces are still blank on the sign-up sheet.
No need to be first, no need to enlarge
The margin of experience beyond what's given.
A life without emulation, a death that's calm
As I accept the end of my many projects
And my dream of heaven. The street
Will survive me. My dust will return to it,
And my soul, too, though smaller than I imagined,
No bigger than a katydid in a bush by a gate
As it helps a yard meet its quota of squeaking.

Distinctions

The world will be no different if the twin sisters
Disputing now in the linen aisle of Kaufmann's
Resolve their difference about table napkins,
Whether the color chosen by one is violet
Or lavender or washed-out purple. No different,
But that's no reason to deem the talk insignificant.
It's important for people to make distinctions,
To want their words to fit appearances snugly.
Why wait to get home before they decide if the napkins
Match the plates Grandmother gave them years back
For their twentieth birthday? A pleasure to hear them,
Like the pleasure of hearing people in a museum
Discuss how closely the landscape approaches
Their notions of the best of the Renaissance
Or would if the paint hadn't cracked in spots
And darkened. Should they deem it fine or very fine
Or remarkable? The world no different but the subject
Not insignificant, the whereabouts of the beautiful,
Just how near it lies to the moment
According to a measurement all can agree on.
That was a beautiful conversation last night
About Vermeer though my friend Ramona
Went off on a tangent, hammering home her theory
As to why he never painted his wife or children.
Could be she was feeling resentful she's only third
On her husband's selective roster of the women
Who've left the deepest marks on his character.
But this morning she may be asking herself what right
She has to complain when he's second on hers,
Below the passionate man she walked away from,
Whose curtain lectures on the plight of Cambodia
Bored her silly. No joy for her, back then,

In loving a man whose conscience burdened itself
With the crimes of others, not simply his own.
Now it seems she lost out on a lucky chance
To widen her heart. However painful that thought,
It's useful when she finds herself too satisfied
With the life she has, forgetting where it fits exactly
On the spectrum of ripeness. Meanwhile, out in her garden,
It's a beautiful morning. The air is a little gritty,
Granted, and the clouds gathering in the west
Have lowered its ranking to seven points out of ten
On the scale of likely prospects. But that doesn't mean
She can't make it a ten on the scale of hope,
Ten for her willingness to be proven wrong.

Two or Three Wishes

Suppose Oedipus never discovers his ignorance
And remains king to the end,
Proud as he walks the streets of Thebes
To think of himself as his city's savior,
The fortunate husband of Queen Jocasta,
The blessed father of two dutiful daughters.
Would we call him happy, a man so unknowing?
If we did, we'd have to admit that happiness
Isn't all we ask for. We want some truth as well,
Whatever that means. We want our notions,
However beautiful and coherent,
Linked to something beyond themselves.
First I want to dream I'm in your thoughts.
Then I want that dream to be a picture
Faithful in flesh and spirit to what is the case.
First I imagine your heart as a city like Thebes
With me as the park you prefer to visit.
Then with my own eyes I want to see you
Resting again and again on one of the benches,
Gathering strength for the messenger
Who may be nearing the outskirts now
Wondering if you'll know how to take the news.

Grace

The thought of the woman you couldn't make happy
Made happy by someone else
Will have to trouble you less than it does now
If you want to disprove the doctrine of the Fall
And enter the world of grace abounding.

On the day you cross the border, you'll be free.
The town she left won't seem so tiny,
The streets so empty and predictable.
Linger too long with your book at dinner
And you'll miss the walk to the river at dusk
When the rare, shy creatures make their appearance.

Then if you walk away from the town's glare
To watch for a few of the brightest stars,
You won't be doing it to impress her,
To prove you can be intimate with the beautiful
Without a craving for ownership.
You'll be enjoying the stars for their own bright sakes.
There they'll be—Vega, Spica, Aldebaran—
High above the sagging roof of a barn.

On the walk back, you'll linger at the outskirts,
Pausing at an open window to listen.
With the radio waves free of the daytime clutter
Talk shows from Phoenix and Memphis will be coming in clear.
Now they seem a mixture of rancor and confusion.
Then they'll sound like half-truths waiting to be fused
By a power within you not yet discovered.

It will be easy then to love the truth
Just for itself, to be content with its cool,

Impersonal light. No need to believe
That your contentment, if she learned of it,
Would give her the pleasure she's always wanted.
You'll want to believe she has pleasure enough
Of her own making, should she need to make it,
Should her new friends prove unreliable.
But if they do, you won't be happy. Not then,
When the sweet water of grace begins to flow.

Bivouac Near Trenton

Now that I see my life composed
Of many stories, not one, I needn't worry so much
If I'll be able to see it whole on my deathbed
With any more certainty than I can now.
A relief not to think of it as a war that hinges
On a final battle after years of skirmishes.
Each day reaches its own conclusions by sundown
About the meaning of freedom, its kinship with loyalty.
And if today the armies of General Washington
Had to stage a retreat, Harlem Heights abandoned,
The soldiers who take each day as it comes
Can be happy they didn't panic.
Now they're falling asleep by the river
In tents or in open air, where I'm ready to join them
As soon as I make my devotions to Night,
The goddess who'll protect this day from invasion,
From any plot hatched by tomorrow.
And now as the tent flap rustles in the wind
I'll finish this letter to you by the fitful candle.
It's cold crossing the Delaware in the grip of winter
And at night it's scary, what with the ice floes.
It's warm inside this letter. No need for mittens.
You were out the day the Declaration inspired me
To declare my independence from the tyrant ambivalence,
Who blocked my pursuit of happiness, so I'm writing.
Night has pulled my phrases beyond revision
Up to the safety of the starry sky
Where Jefferson's silvery phrases twinkle untarnished,
Untouched by the story that he died in debt,
Beloved Monticello taken by creditors,
The slaves sold he'd hoped to free.

Consolation

Could be, she tells herself, the Brahmins are right
And she's enjoyed already, in a past existence,
The life that for years she's lamented missing,
Already driven home with her heart's companion,
Who in this existence is driving with someone else.
Already been welcomed by their ducks and dogs
And shared over dinner their plans for tomorrow.
Could be that what tastes to her like longing
Is really memory, the trace not washed from her tongue
When she kneeled to sip the dark water of Lethe.
That's why the house in the country where he lives now
Looked so familiar the one time she dared to pass it,
A weathered farmhouse in the shingle style
Set back from the road in a rising field.
She must have lived there once, a good life,
No doubt about it, selected by her watchful soul,
Who wants the best for her, as this life has been selected,
This climbing the stairs to her city apartment
A block from the discount store, her arms full of groceries.
Already she's planning her project when dinner's done.
This could be the night at her writing desk
When she breaks through the walls of the well-made story
And flows with a loose, associative style
Out to the hollows and crevices of experience.
Her old life won't get her there, to this discovery,
However much she may have learned with her friend
As she read to him on the couch by the stove
Or listened to his reading and commentary.
Does she want to repeat herself, she asks, or move on?
To say she was happier then than now,
To say she's more restless now, and lonely,
Could mean, if the Brahmins are right,

She's stuck in the fiction of the one best life,
Mired in the language of ranking, while the questing soul
Needs many lives to complete its journey,
Each with its own definition of happiness.
The current definition could emerge tonight
As she sits at her desk shaping her thoughts into unity
Long past the hour when her heart's companion
Has gone to bed with his sweetheart to whisper and touch
As once she may have whispered and touched
In a life with him she's promised herself
Not to dwell on now.

Writing at Night

This empty feeling that makes me fearful
I'll disappear the minute I stop thinking
May only mean that beyond the kitchen window, in the dark,
The minions of the past are gathering,
Waiting for the dishes to be cleared away
So they can hustle supper into oblivion.

This feeling may only mean that supper's done
And night has the house surrounded
And the past is declaring itself the victor.
It doesn't deny that tomorrow I'll wake to find
That the usual bales of light have been unloaded
And distributed equally in every precinct,
That the tree at the corner is awash in it
And the flaming, yellow coats of the crossing guards.

This empty feeling could be a gift
I haven't yet grown used to, a lightness
That means I've shaken off the weight of resentment,
Envy, remorse, and pride that drags the soul down.
A thinness that lets me slip through a needle's eye
Into the here and now of the kitchen.
Without losing a button.

An emptiness that betokens a talent for self-forgetting
That lets me welcome the stories of others,
Which even now may be on their way,
Hoping I'll take them in however rumpled they look
And gray-faced as they drag themselves from the car

With their bulky night bags and water jugs.
It's late. Have I gone to bed? they wonder.
And then they see the light in the kitchen
And a figure who could be me at the table
Still up writing.

As If

Before dawn, while you're still sleeping,
Playing the part of a dreamer whose house is an ark
Tossed about by a flood that will never subside,
Its dove doomed to return with no twig,
Your neighbor's already up, pulling his boots on,
Playing the part of a fisherman,
Gathering gear and loading his truck
And driving to the river and wading in
As if fishing is all he's ever wanted.

Three trout by the time you get up and wash
And come to breakfast served by a woman who smiles
As if you're first on her short list of wonders,
And you greet her as if she's first on yours.
Then you're off to school to fulfill your promise
To lose yourself for once in your teaching
And forget the clock facing your desk. Time to behave
As if the sun's standing still in a painted sky
And the day isn't a page in a one-page notebook
To be filled by sundown or never filled,
First the lines and then the margins,
The words jammed in till no white shows.

And while you're speaking as if everyone's listening,
A mile from school, at the city hall,
The mayor is behaving as if it matters
That the blueprints drawn up for the low-rent housing
Include the extra windows he's budgeted,
That the architects don't transfer the funds
To shutters and grates as they did last year
But understand that brightness is no extravagance.
And when lunch interrupts him, it's a business lunch

To plan the autumn parade, as if the fate of the nation
Hangs on keeping the floats of the poorer precincts
From looking skimpy and threadbare.

The strollers out on the street today
Don't have to believe all men are created equal,
All endowed by their creator with certain rights,
As long as they behave as if they do,
As if they believe the country will be better off
If more people do likewise, that acting this way
May help their fellow Americans better pursue
The happiness your housemate believes she's pursuing
By sharing her house with you, that the fisherman
Wants to believe he's found in fishing.

Now while you're thinking you can make her happy
As long as she's willing to behave as if you can
The fisherman keeps so still on his log
As he munches a biscuit that the fish
Rise to the surface to share his crumbs.
And the heron stands on the sandbank silently staring
As if it's wondering what the man is thinking,
Its gray eyes glinting like tin or glass.

Starry Night

Only a few stars are visible when I step outside
For a walk to the mailbox with my packet of poems.
In a week or two Mary will take time out
From preparing her class on Melville
To mark the lines that seem to need more work.
If I don't agree with her now, it's likely I will
In a month or two when I gain more distance.
Are other writers as lucky in their friends as I am
Or do they go it alone, as Melville did?
To get some distance on *Billy Budd,* he left the manuscript
Untouched for six months in the dark of a desk drawer,
The last six months of his life, it turned out.
Maybe he was planning to go back to it
For a final review and then search for a publisher
If publishing still mattered to him
And he thought a story so far from the fashion
For middling characters could find a public.
A book so different from the one I'm writing,
The way it reveals its truth in extremes.
How boldly Melville likens his sailor hero
To Adam before the Fall and then to Jesus.
On the lid of the box that held the papers
He pasted the words, "Be true to the dreams of thy youth."
And if he felt true, as is likely, what more did he need?
Here is the mailbox, and this is the comforting sound
Of my packet of poems hitting the bottom.
And now it's time to walk back under the streetlights,
Wondering what a youthful dream of adventure
Would conclude if it could see me,
How much explaining it would ask me for
And how much revision, if it thought revision
One of the choices still available.

Still Life

Now's a good time, before the night comes on,
To praise the loyalty of the vase of flowers
Gracing the parlor table, and the bowl of oranges,
And the book with freckled pages resting on the tablecloth.
To remark how these items aren't conspiring
To pack their bags and move to a place
Where stillness appears to more advantage.
No plan for a heaven above, beyond, or within,
Whose ever-blooming bushes are rustling
In a sea breeze at this very moment.
These items are focusing all their attention
On holding fast as time washes around them.
The flowers in the vase won't come again.
The page of the book beside it, the edge turned down,
Will never be read again for the first time.
The light from the window's angled.
The sun's moving on. That's why the people
Who live in the house are missing.
They're all outside enjoying the light that's left them.
Lucky for them to find when they return
These silent things just as they were.
Night's coming on and they haven't been frightened off.
They haven't once dreamed of going anywhere.

Your City

How much would it take for this city
That so far has belonged to others
To be yours as well,
The houses set in rows and each row named
So you can find the garden of your new acquaintance
Long before sundown, just as you promised,
And the talk has time to wander and pause.

How much as you walk home in the dark
For the portly policeman, who now
Stands on the corner for others,
To stand for you by the grocery store
Still open for your convenience,
The lettuce and cucumber planted last spring
For you as well, weeded and watered,
Picked this very week, sorted and loaded,
And driven along a highway where a highway crew
Has worked all month for you digging a culvert.

How much for the book on the nightstand at home,
Written now for others, to be written for you
In hours stolen from sleep and children,
Sweet and bitter wisdom distilled as a gift
As the author guesses you'll be coming along
In need of encouragement and of warning.

Three weeks till it's due at the local library.
How much would it take for the right
To wander the stacks all afternoon,
Wrested for others from kings and shamans,
To be wrested for you as well,
And the Constitution amended to protect your rights

Against the privileges of the few
And the prejudice of the many.

You learned the story in school but couldn't believe it.
How much would it take for it all to be possible,
To walk the streets of a glimmering city
Begemmed with houses of worship and lecture halls
That thrust the keys to bliss into your hands.
A city where for you as well
Mohammed decides to linger at Mecca
And Jesus rides his donkey into crazed Jerusalem
And Moses descends the mountain and loving Buddha
Turns his back on heaven, hearing your sighs.

How long a wait till invisible hands,
That have left instructions for others
In every lonely hotel room, lead you
To lock up evil and coax the good
From whatever corner of your soul it's fled to,
The beleaguered good you've always imagined
Looking for others to deliver it
When all along it's looked for you.

from
Practical Gods
(2001)

A Priest of Hermes

The way up, from here to there, may be closed,
But the way down, from there to here, still open
Wide enough for a slender god like Hermes
To slip from the clouds if you give your evenings
To learning about the plants under his influence,
The winged and wingless creatures, the rocks and metals,
And practice his sacred flute or dulcimer.

No prayers. Just the effort to make his stay
So full of the comforts of home he won't forget it,
To build him a shrine he finds congenial,
Something as simple as roofed pillars
Without the darkness of an interior.

If you're lucky, he'll want to sit on the steps
Under the stars for as long as you live
And sniff the fragrance of wine and barley
As it blows from the altar on a salty sea breeze.
He'll want, when you die, to offer his services
As a guide on the shadowy path to the underworld.

Not till you reach the watery crossing
Will he leave your side, and even then
He'll shout instructions as you slip from your shoes
And wade alone into that dark river.

Saint Francis and the Nun

The message Saint Francis preached to the birds,
Though not recorded, isn't beyond surmising.
He wanted his fellow creatures to taste the joy
Of singing the hymns he sang on waking,
Hymns of thanksgiving that praised creation.
Granted, the birds had problems with comprehension,
But maybe they'd grasp enough of his earnest tone
To feel that spring shouldn't be taken lightly.
An audience hard to hold, to be sure,
With a narrow attention span, a constant fluttering,
But a lot less challenging than the nun he counseled
Only this morning, a woman still young,
Dying slowly in pain, who asked him
Why if her suffering had a purpose
That purpose couldn't be clarified in a vision.
Why not at least some evidence
That the greater the suffering reserved for her
The smaller the portion reserved for others?
What a balm to be able to think as Jesus did,
That with every difficult breath of hers
Patients in sickbeds around the world
Suddenly found they were breathing easier.
What a relief for Saint Francis these birds are,
Free of the craving for explanation, for certainty
Even in winter, when the grass is hidden. "Look!"
He calls to them, pointing. "Those black specks
There in the snow are seed husks. Think
As you circle down how blessed you are."
But what can he point to in the nun's spare cell
To keep her from wondering why it's so hard
For the king of heaven to comfort her?
All she can manage now is to hope for the will

Not to abandon her god, if he is her god,
In his hour of weakness. No time to reply
To the tender homily at her bedside
As she gathers all her strength for the end,
Hoping to cry out briefly as Jesus did
When his body told him he was on his own.

Department Store

"Thou shalt not covet," hardest of the Commandments,
Is listed last so the others won't be neglected.
An hour a day of practice is all that anyone
Can expect you to spare, and in ten years' time
You may find you've outgrown your earlier hankering
For your neighbor's house, though his is brick
And yours is clapboard, though his contains a family.
Ten years of effort and finally it's simple justice
To reward yourself with a token of self-approval.

Stand tall as you linger this evening
In the sweater section of Kaufmann's Department Store
By the case for men not afraid of extravagance.
All will go well if you hold your focus steady
On what's before you and cast no covetous eye
On the middle-aged man across the aisle
In women's accessories as he converses quietly
With his teenaged son. The odds are slim
They're going to reach agreement about a gift
Likely to please the woman they live with,
Not with the clash in what they're wearing,
The father dapper in sport coat and tie, the son
Long-haired, with a ring in his ear and a shirt
That might have been worn by a Vandal chieftain
When he torched a town at the edge of the Empire.

This moment you covet is only a truce
In a lifelong saga of border warfare
While each allows the other with a shake of the head
To veto a possibility as they slowly progress
From umbrellas to purses, from purses to gloves
In search of something bright for the darker moments

When the woman realizes her life with them
Is the only life she'll be allotted.

It's only you who assumes the relief on their faces
When they hold a scarf to the light and nod
Will last. The boy will have long forgotten this moment
Years from now when the woman he's courting
Asks him to name a happy time with his dad,
A time of peaceable parley amidst the turmoil.
So why should you remember? Think how angry
You'll be at yourself tomorrow if you let their purchase
Make you unhappy with yours, ashamed
Of a sweater on sale that fits you well,
Gray-blue, your favorite color.

Not the Idle

It's not the idle who move us but the few
Often confused with the idle, those who define
Their project in life in terms so ample
Nothing they ever do is a digression.
Each episode contributes its own rare gift
As a chapter in *Moby-Dick* on squid or hardtack
Is just as important to Ishmael as a fight with a whale.
The few who refuse to live for the plot's sake,
Major or minor, but for texture and tone and hue.
For them weeding a garden all afternoon
Can't be construed as a detour from the road of life.
The road narrows to a garden path that turns
And circles to show that traveling goes only so far
As a metaphor. The day rests on the grass.
And at night the books of these few,
Lined up on their desks, don't look like drinks
Lined up on a bar to help them evade their troubles.
They look like an escort of mountain guides
Come to conduct the climber to a lofty outlook
Rising serene above the fog. For them the view
Is no digression though it won't last long
And they won't remember even the vivid details.
The supper with friends back in the village
In a dining room brightened with flowers and paintings
No digression for them, though the talk leads
To no breakthrough. The topic they happen to hit on
Isn't a ferry to carry them over the interval
Between soup and salad. It's a raft drifting downstream
Where the banks widen to embrace a lake
And birds rise from the reeds in many colors.
Everyone tries to name them and fails
For an hour no one considers idle.

Gelati

These songs from the corner church,
Wafting through the window this August morning,
Lift the job of sanding my scarred oak bookcase
From a three, on a ten-point scale of joy,
To at least a four. Not a bad grade
For an enterprise mainly practical, preparing a site
Fittingly handsome for the noble shelf-load
Of Roman Stoics whose sensible pages,
Stacked now on my speakers, don't register on the joy chart.
A cold wind blows from their doctrine that a virtuous life
Is in harmony with the cosmos—the cold, companionless cosmos
That never comes through when you need a friend.
No wonder the early Christians won followers.
No wonder their living descendants sound joyful still
As they proclaim that even here, near the corner
Of Hodge and Elmwood, the soul may be quickened.

These singers have had a brush with vision
Denied me so far, though once, on the Appian Way,
Three miles outside of Rome, after I'd walked for hours,
Inspecting the roadside tombs, alone, in the heat of August,
Wishing I'd brought a water jug, ready to turn back,
A man pushing a cart suddenly staged an advent
As he intoned, *"Limonata, gelati,"* as if to a crowd
Though the road was empty. An old man
With a bright escutcheon of ice cream staining his apron,
Proclaiming that to ask is to have for the lucky few
Who know what to ask for.

For a minute it seemed the Bureau of Joy was calling
About a windfall blowing my way to guarantee
An eight or nine on the joy chart even if many wishes

Down on my list wouldn't be granted.
Today I seem to be focusing on my wish to sand
And stain and varnish my bookcase, a job that a monk
Who specializes in repetition might embrace as a ritual.
Let the moment expand, he says to himself,
Till time is revealed to be delusion.

For me, here in the passing hour,
The wind-borne singing brightens the moment
However faintly it enters, however it might be improved
By the brighter acoustics of the New Jerusalem.
And now it's time for a string quartet in a new recording.
And now it's time for the baseball game on the radio.

Whether the players regard the sport as joy
Or simply as work, the crowd seems alive
With the wish to compress a lifetime
Down to a single sitting. Now for the task
Of brushing the varnish on with a steady hand
While the crowd goes wild in the bottom of the ninth
As the man on first steps off the bag, a rookie
Who'll seem a savior if he gets home.

To a Pagan

It's sad to see you offer your prayers to the sun god
And then, when you really need him, discover too late
That though he's willing to help, other gods more potent
Decide against him. It's too late then to regret
You didn't invest your trust where we've invested.

Join us, and if help doesn't arrive at once,
At least the deputy angel assigned your district
May hear your groans in the wind and track them
Down to your attic apartment in the outskirts
And mark the coordinates on her map.

Then she's off on the long trek through the voids
To report the crisis. Imagine the vault of the stars
As a tundra stretching away for a million miles
Without so much as a hut for shelter,
Without a tree or a bush for a windbreak.

Imagine how lonely she is as she builds a fire
Of tundra grass in the mouth of a cave,
A fire that proves too small and smoky
To warm her icy plumage. Then add her voice
As she quakes a psalm to keep up her spirits.

Dwelling on her, your heart will fill with compassion
And you'll want to cry out, "Great friend, I'm thankful
For all you suffer for my sake, but I'm past help.
Help someone more likely to benefit," the prayer
Of a real convert, which is swiftly answered.

History

I too could give my heart to history.
I too could turn to it for illumination,
For a definition of who we are, what it means to live here
Breathing this atmosphere at the end of the century.
I too could agree we aren't pilgrims
Resting for the night at a roadside hermitage,
Uncertain about the local language and customs,
But more like the bushes and trees around us,
Sprung from this soil, nurtured by the annual rainfall
And the slant of the sun in our temperate latitudes.

If only history didn't side with survivors,
The puny ones who in times of famine
Can live on nothing, or the big and greedy.
If only it didn't conclude that the rebels who take the fort
Must carry the flag of the future in their knapsacks
While the rebels who fail have confused their babble
With the voice of the people, which announces by instinct
The one and only path to posterity.

The people are far away in the provinces
With their feet on the coffee table
Leafing through magazines on barbecuing and sailing.
They're dressing to go to an uncle's funeral,
To a daughter's rehearsal dinner. They're listening,
As they drive to work, to the radio.
Caesar's ad on law and order seems thoughtful.
Brutus's makes some useful points about tyranny.
But is either candidate likely to keep his promises?

When ice floes smashed the barges on the Delaware
And Washington drowned with all his men, it was clear

To the world the revolt he led against excise taxes
And import duties was an overreaction.
When the South routed the North at Gettysburg
It was clear the scheme of merchants to impose their values
On cotton planters was doomed from the start
Along with Lincoln's mystical notion of union,
Which sadly confused the time-bound world we live in
With a world where credos don't wear out.

School Days

On the heart's map of the country, a thousand miles
May be represented by a quarter inch, the distance
Between St. Louis and a boarding school in Massachusetts
Where the son will be taught by the same teachers
Who taught his father and will reappear Christmas
At Union Station singing his father's songs.

Likewise the distance walked by an immigrant mother
From the tenement on Locust to the school on Seventh
Equals the distance on the heart's map of the world
Between the Volga and the Mississippi.

Now she's left the children at the school door
And has watched them enter a country she'll never visit
From which they'll return this evening with stories
She won't be able to understand. And on weekends,
When she and her husband fill their one big room
With the clatter of piecework, the children wait for a seat
In the reading room of the Cass Avenue library
Where a book is a ship, its prow pointed toward Ithaca.

A thousand kisses to you, Miss Winslow, senior librarian,
With a slice of poppy-seed cake that Mother made
For your help in boarding and raising the sails.
Now for the lotus-eaters and witches, princesses, gods,
Not one of which leaves Odysseus at a loss for words.
And all the words in English, a language stiff as a stone
On the tongue of the oldsters but flexible for the children.

What skill could be more useful than making a stranger
A friend with a single speech or tricking a giant
Eager to eat you? The boring parts can be skimmed

Like the trip to shadow land, where the hero has to sit still
And listen to the sad stories of shadows.

Three times he tries to embrace his mother,
Who pined away with longing for her lone son
Wandering far from home, buffeted by the sea god.
Three times he embraces only air.

Prophet

You'll never be much of a prophet if, when the call comes
To preach to Nineveh, you flee on the ship for Tarshish
That Jonah fled on, afraid like him of the people's outrage
Were they to hear the edict that in thirty days
Their city in all its glory will be overthrown.

The sea storm that harried Jonah won't harry you.
No big fish will be waiting to swallow you whole
And keep you down in the dark till your mood
Shifts from fear to thankfulness and you want to serve.
No. You'll land safe at Tarshish and learn the language
And get a job in a countinghouse by the harbor
And marry and raise a family you can be proud of
In a neighborhood not too rowdy for comfort.

If you're going to be a prophet, you must listen the first time.
Setting off at sunrise, you can't be disheartened
If you arrive at Nineveh long past midnight,
On foot, your donkey having run off with your baggage.
You'll have to settle for a room in the cheapest hotel
And toss all night on the lice-ridden mattress

That Jonah is spared. In the space of three sentences
He jumps from his donkey, speaks out, and is heeded, while you,
Preaching next day in the rain on a noisy corner,
Are likely to be ignored, outshouted by old-clothes dealers
And fishwives, mocked by schoolboys for your accent.
And then it's a week in jail for disturbing the peace.
There you'll have time, as you sit in a dungeon

Darker than a whale's belly, to ask if the trip
Is a big mistake, the heavenly voice mere mood,

The mission a fancy. Jonah's biggest complaint
Is that God, when the people repent and ask forgiveness,
Is glad to forgive them and cancels the doomsday
Specified in the prophecy, leaving his prophet
To look like a fool. So God takes time to explain
How it's wrong to want a city like this one to burn,
How a prophet's supposed to redeem the future,
Not predict it. But you'll be left with the question
Why your city's been spared when nobody's different,

Nobody in the soup kitchen you open,
Though one or two of the hungriest
May be grateful enough for the soup to listen
When you talk about turning their lives around.
It will be hard to believe these are the saving remnant
Kin to the ten just men who would have sufficed
To save Gomorrah if Abraham could have found them.

You'll have to tell them frankly you can't explain
Why Nineveh is still standing though you hope to learn
At the feet of a prophet who for all you know
May be turning his donkey toward Nineveh even now.

Delphi

Though I don't believe in oracles, I'm encouraged
By those who do, by their certainty that the future,
However narrow, isn't so closed as the past.
Options appear to persist for the passengers
Disembarking at the port of Corinth, persist as they rest
Before the jolting donkey ride up the mountain
And the long wait for their turn on the porch of the temple.

The farmer fresh from his farm on the island of Melos
Can't predict what the priestess will answer
When asked the wisest policy toward his son,
Though he knows what he wants her to say:
That the boy has studied enough in Athens,
That another year means losing him to philosophy
When he ought to be home to help with the harvest.

The father listens with a mind as open
As he can make it when Apollo's servant,
Her eyes shut tight, her lips foam-flecked,
Mutters and moans in a voice not hers
Words that even to her are a mystery.

As for me, my only oracle is my notebook
Open on the kitchen table to a page divided
Straight down the middle with a heavy line.
If the arguments on the left-hand side
Outnumber those on the right, the left-hand path
At the fork ahead should be my preference
Unless the arguments on the right, however few,
Appear more beautiful, their truth more piercing.

And wouldn't that difference mean
That the right-hand path is the one I believe
An oracle would confirm if oracles existed?
The path that would lead me to the brighter good,
Me and the rest of the world worth helping,
My first choice, not my distant second.

Pride

A danger on many lists, but on mine
The best protection I have when I get an inkling
Of what it means to be shut forever
Inside one person, the windows barred.
Pride that proclaims to me and my kind
That the self isn't so small as it seems,
Just the small corner we're standing in,
Just this moment, which contains only a fraction
Of all we are. Look up, says pride, at the misty ceiling;
Look up ahead where the far wall rises
Covered with tapestries it will take a lifetime
To admire with the focused attention that they deserve.

Take pride away, and envy would scale our ramparts
Unopposed and force us to sign the papers
Declaring the rooms of houses other than ours
Far more inviting, more spacious and sunny,
The furniture chosen with taste that we can't muster,
The guests over there not only more interesting
But more generous than the tribe of gossips
And climbers crowding our anterooms.

O pride, O sweet assurance we're first,
May the dreams you provide us with always allow us
To ride in triumph through a grateful Persepolis
Certain we've earned the shouts of the crowd,
Certain the queen by our side isn't deluded
To love us best, just enlightened beyond her years.
Her gaze pierces to a trove of virtues
Hidden even from us, and will teach us
How wrong we've been to consider her heart
More cramped in its movements now that it beats for us,
Now that it's ours.

On the Bus to Utica

Up to a year ago I'd have driven myself to Utica
As I've always done when visiting Aunt Jeannine.
But since last summer, and the bad experience in my car
With aliens, I prefer bus travel. Do you believe
In creatures more advanced than we are
Visiting now and then from elsewhere in the universe?
Neither did I till experience taught me otherwise.
It happened one night last fall after the Rotary meeting.
I'd lingered, as chapter chairman, to sort my notes,
So I wasn't surprised when I finally got to the lot
To find my car the only one there, though the shadows
Hovering over it should have been a tip-off
And the strong odor I had trouble placing—
Salty, ashy, metallic. My thoughts were elsewhere,
Reliving the vote at the meeting to help a restaurant
Take its first steps in a risky neighborhood.
So the element of surprise was theirs, the four of them,
Three who pulled me in when I opened the door
And one who drove us out past the town edge
To a cleared field where a three-legged landing craft
Big as a moving van sat idling. In its blue-green light
I caught my first good look at their faces. Like ours,
But with eyes bigger and glossier, and foreheads bumpier
With bristles from the eyebrows up, the hair of hedgehogs.
No rudeness from them, no shouting or shoving.
Just quiet gestures signaling me to sit down
And keep calm as we rose in silence to the mother ship.
I remember the red lights of the docking platform,
A dark hall, a room with a gurney where it dawned on me
Just before I went under there would be no discussions,
No sharing of thoughts on the fate of the universe,
No messages to bring back to my fellow earthlings.

When I woke from the drug they'd dosed me with
I was back in the car, in the Rotary parking lot,
With a splitting headache and a feeling I'd been massaged
Hard for a week or two by giants. Now I feel fine
Though my outlook on life has altered. It rankles
To think that beings have reached us who are smugly certain
All they can learn from us is what we can learn
From dissecting sea worms or banding geese.
Let's hope their science is pure at least,
Not a probe for a colony in the Milky Way.
Do you think they've planted a bug inside me?
Is that why you're silent? Fear will do us more harm
Than they will. Be brave. Be open.
Tell me something you won't confide to your friends
Out of fear they may think you strange, eccentric.
If you're waiting for an audience that's more congenial,
More sensitive than the one that happens
To be sitting beside you now on this ramshackle bus,
I can sympathize. Once I waited too.
Now you can see I take what's offered.

Jesus Freaks

The approval they get from above is all they need,
So why should they care if they offend me
Here in the parking lot of the Super Duper, my arms full,
By stuffing a pamphlet or two in my pocket?

No point in shouting at them to keep back
When they're looking for disapproval. No reason
For them to obey the rules of one of the ignorant
Who supposes the perpetual dusk he lives in

Sunny noon. Their business is with my soul,
However buried, with my unvoiced wish for the truth
Too soft for me to catch over the street noise.
Should I rest my packages on my car a minute

And try to listen if I'm sure they really believe
They're vexing me in my own best interest?
To them I'm the loser they used to be
When they sweated daily to please themselves,

Deaf to their real wishes. Why make it easy for me
To load the trunk of my car with grocery bags
When they offer a joy that none of my purchases,
However free of impurities, can provide?

Their calls to attention shouldn't sound any more threatening
Than the peal of a church bell. And if I call
On the car phone to lodge a complaint,
Jail will seem to them the perfect place to bear witness

In this dark dominion where Herod rules.
In jail, but also guests at a banquet, while I,

They're certain, stubbornly stand outside
Shivering in the snow, too proud

To enter a hall not of my own devising
And warm myself at a fire I didn't light
And enjoy a meal strangers have taken pains with.
Yes, the table's crowded, but there's room for me.

The Serpent to Adam

Just as Prometheus, the compassionate god,
Stole to deliver man from darkness,
So for your welfare I named the forbidden tree
The tree of knowledge. And just as he understood
The punishment that was bound to follow,
The rules of Olympus being clearly posted,
So I was ready to drag my trunk through the dust
Toward the glow of your first campfire.
My loss would be far outmatched by the joy
I'd feel in the company of my new-made equals.
At last a chance for serious conversation
As we planned together a home in the wilderness
Fit for creatures who know good from evil.

No wonder I was stunned by your kicks and curses.
No wonder I was wounded in more than body
As I scuttled back to the dark, dodging your stones.
Nothing could ever make you happy again
Now that the gardener didn't dote on you
And you'd have to fend for yourself,
Grow your own food and cook it,
Standing close to the fire to fend off cold.

That was your real crime, not disobedience:
To make me, a being hopeful by nature,
Into a slinking creature of holes and crevices,
My talents wasted, my soul so embittered
I was glad when I lost my lizard ears.
A relief not to hear anymore your wind-borne
Misty laments from the valley settlements.
A thousand sighs for an Eden that didn't suit you
And none for the Eden we might have made.

View of Delft

In the view of Delft that Vermeer presents us
The brick façades of the unremarkable buildings
Lined up at the river's edge manage to lift the spirits
Though the sky is cloudy. A splash of sun
That yellows some gables in the middle distance
May be enough to explain it, or the loving detail
Vermeer has given the texture of brick and stone
As if he leveled each course with his own trowel.
Doubtless stones in Cleveland or Buffalo
May look like this on a day when the news arrives
That a friend is coming to visit, but the stones in the painting
Also put one in mind of the New Jerusalem,
A city we've never seen and don't believe in.
Why eternal Jerusalem when the people of Delft
Grow old and die as they do in other cities,
In high-ceilinged airy rooms and in low-beamed
Smoky basements, quickly, or after a stubborn illness,
Alone, or surrounded by friends who will soon feel Delft
To be a place of abandonment, not completion?
Maybe to someone returning on a cloudy day
After twenty years of banishment the everyday buildings
Can look this way or to someone about to leave
On a journey he isn't ready to take. But these moods
Won't last long while the mood in the painting
Seems undying, though the handful of citizens
Strolling the other side of the river are too preoccupied
To look across and admire their home.
Vermeer has to know that the deathless city
Isn't the Delft where he'll be walking to dinner
In an hour or two. As for your dinner, isn't it time
To close the art book you've been caught up in,
Fetch a bottle of wine from the basement, and stroll

Three blocks to the house where your friend is waiting?
Don't be surprised if the painting lingers awhile in memory
And the trees set back on a lawn you're passing
Seem to say that to master their language of gestures
Is to learn all you need to know to enter your life
And embrace it tightly, with a species of joy
You've yet to imagine. But this joy, disguised,
The painting declares, is yours already.
You've been longing again for what you have.

A Chance for the Soul

Am I leading the life that my soul,
Mortal or not, wants me to lead is a question
That seems at least as meaningful as the question
Am I leading the life I want to live,
Given the vagueness of the pronoun "I,"
The number of things it wants at any moment.

Fictive or not, the soul asks for a few things only,
If not just one. So life would be clearer
If it weren't so silent, inaudible
Even here in the yard an hour past sundown
When the pair of cardinals and crowd of starlings
Have settled down for the night in the poplars.

Have I planted the seed of my talent in fertile soil?
Have I watered and trimmed the sapling?
Do birds nest in my canopy? Do I throw a shade
Others might find inviting? These are some handy metaphors
The soul is free to use if it finds itself
Unwilling to speak directly for reasons beyond me,
Assuming it's eager to be of service.

Now the moon, rising above the branches,
Offers itself to my soul as a double,
Its scarred face an image of the disappointment
I'm ready to say I've caused if the soul
Names the particulars and suggests amendments.

So fine are the threads that the moon
Uses to tug at the ocean that Galileo himself
Couldn't imagine them. He tried to explain the tides
By the earth's momentum as yesterday

I tried to explain my early waking
Three hours before dawn by street noise.

Now I'm ready to posit a tug
Or nudge from the soul. Some insight
Too important to be put off till morning
Might have been mine if I'd opened myself
To the occasion as now I do.

Here's a chance for the soul to fit its truth
To a world of yards, moons, poplars, and starlings,
To resist the fear that to talk my language
Means to be shoehorned into my perspective
Till it thinks as I do, narrowly.

"Be brave, Soul," I want to say to encourage it.
"Your student, however slow, is willing,
The only student you'll ever have."

Audience

When I take the time to read slowly, the words sink in.
If I hadn't rushed my reading of *Anna Karenina*
The first time through, focusing on plot, not nuance,
I might have been able to say why Karenin,
On the night he discovers his wife loves Vronsky,
Gives her a cool lecture on the proprieties
And hides what he feels, how the bridge of his life
Has suddenly fallen away beneath him.
Why does a man who's tumbling into the void
Want to tumble in silence, without a cry?

Now as I drive to visit a friend in the country,
Listening as the story is slowly spoken on tape
By an actress with all the time in the world,
It's clear to me the invisible beings
Karenin imagines watching him from their balcony
Would be embarrassed by any display of feeling.

As to why he's chosen for himself an audience
That judges on the basis of a cool appearance,
Good form, good show, and neglects the soul,
This must be what it means to live in St. Petersburg,
City of courtiers and court ambitions,
And not in Moscow, its country cousin,
Noisy with laughing and crying families.

I'm glad the friend I'm driving to visit
Lives hours away in a country village,
A tolerant woman who won't reproach me

For driving slowly, who'll be glad to learn
I'm taking my own sweet time for reflection.

It's a shame no one enlightened steps forward
To tell Karenin he's a character in a novel
Where no one's commended for preserving his dignity,
Only for shouting and weeping and tearing his hair,
For throwing a book of philosophy out the window.

It looks like I'm one of the fortunate few
With leisure enough to ask myself
If all the invisible beings watching my life
Hail from Moscow. And I'll have time this evening
To ask my friend her honest opinion
And to weigh her answer.
And then it's time to ask if the life she's living
Pleases the beings she imagines watching
And whether they watch from duty or sympathy.

Life would be easier, I'll say, if our audience
Were a single person, like Dante's Beatrice.
Just the thought of her silently looking on
From across a stream was enough to brighten a path
Otherwise forlorn. But how can Dante be sure,
My friend will ask me, that he knows her wishes?
What if they don't all show in her face, or only show
As if veiled by mist, and he sees them darkly?

A Letter from Mary in the Tyrol

You may believe you're as sorry as you say you are
Not to be hiking with me over mountain meadows,
Sorry your duties at home keep you from travel.
Still, I have to admit I was tempted this afternoon,
As I stood in a guildhall square by a clock tower,
To liken you to the painted soldier
Lurching from his house high in the clock face
To tap the rim of his drum two times.

He looked so full of his mission, so solemn,
As if without his efforts the dome of the sky,
Turning too slow or fast, would begin to wobble,
And crack in the middle, and come crashing down.

All around him the visible face of the landscape
Cried out for attention, the cry I've been hearing
These last few days and answering as best I can
Without the contributions you might have made.

At least I haven't distracted myself from the moment
With thinking of projects I've left half-finished.
At least I know my friends can get on without me,
The gap I've left in their days already closing
While I give my attention to vistas
Far more flamboyant than I imagined.

As I left the square to walk the ramparts,
The soldier was jerking back to his tin house
For another hour of practice.

Three o'clock would be here,
With all its responsibilities, before he knew it.

Is it fair to liken his theory of time to yours?
To me you seem to regard a day as water
Dripping from your cupped fingers,
Each drop a loss you'll have to account for
On the day of judgment you say you don't believe in.

Everyone, to be sure, can use a metaphor.
I don't deny I want to believe this landscape
Has been waiting eons for eyes like mine,
As tender and clear and steady,
And has taken a vow to hold back nothing.

There's nothing wrong with imagining missions
So long as we understand why we choose them,
And approve our motives, and debate alternatives.
Consider our brother in his windowless tin house,
The good it would do him to ask why it seems so fine,
When he could be elsewhere, to wait in the dark,
Shoulders thrown back, for his cue.

Numbers

Two hands may not always be better than one,
But four feet and more are likely to prove
More steady than two as we wade a stream
Holding above our heads the ark
Of our covenant with the true and beautiful,
A crowd of outlaw pagans hot on our heels,
The shades of our ancestors cheering us on.

Three friends with poems at Mac's this evening
Are closer than one to the truth if we lift our glasses
To the poet that Mac proposes
We toast before beginning, Li Po.

Three votes that the poem I've brought is finished
Versus one turn of the head too slight
For anyone not on the watch to notice
As Li Po demurs.

Is this America, land of one man, one vote,
I want to ask, or the China of one-man rule,
Of emperors who believe they're gods?

Li Po, now only a thin layer of dust
In Szechwan Province though somehow
Still standing inches behind his words.

Five of my lines, he suggests with a nod,
Out of the score I've written,
Are fine as they are if I provide them

The context that they deserve and speak them
Without misgivings and with greater gusto.

Five lead out from the kitchen
Past a dozen detours to a single bridge
That must be crossed in order to reach a homeland
Eager for my arrival.

This is the message I get from a prophet whose signs
Are a threadbare coat and an empty cupboard,
Proof he's never written for anyone but himself
And the dead teachers easy to count
On the stiff fingers of one hand.

IN MEMORY OF MAC HAMMOND

The Fallen

Now that a year's gone by since your enemy
From childhood on, implacable diabetes,
Finally defeated you, it's time for you to appear
In dream, your sight restored, your indignant beard
Peaceably trimmed, your prophet's brow,
Creased before by the world's injustices,
Smooth as you take a chair at my bedside.

You'll have come to tell me the relief I felt
When your heart gave out after a day at the hospital
Was only natural, natural for a friend
Who was glad you'd given the slip at last
To a body that was never loyal,
To a servant plotting still more betrayals.

With a doctor's graceful bedside manner, you'll say
That if I begrudged you an extra portion of sympathy
I have nothing to be ashamed of.
Your loneliness must have felt to me like a pit
Too vast to be filled, while duties more doable
Called for attention, and I wanted to make a difference,
To see in people around me proof of my power.

There's a time for remorse, your ghost will explain,
And a time to believe the future offers occasions
More ample than those yet offered
For making improvements and moving on.

I'm listening to the speech I'm having you make
About the forgiveness filling your heart
Even if I was common enough to wish
Simply to spend my leisure in cheerier company,

With friends less retrospective, distant, and death-bound.
You're linking my lapse to the lapse that Milton, your hero,
Attributed to the pair who brought Eden down.

The will, I'm waiting for you to say, is composed
Of many voices, and of these only one
Can be labeled fallen, one selfish voice
Clamoring for the floor in the chamber of voices
When the soul convenes far enough from the street
To hear itself debating.

Just one sleek speaker who argues the point
That the suffering overseas is a quagmire
Best avoided, however pure our intentions.
A voice that more often than not
Fails to persuade the others, and when it succeeds
Leaves them all feeling small and stingy.

IN MEMORY OF BURTON WEBER

Eurydice

If the dead could speak, I'd entreat you
Not to blame yourself for losing me near the exit.
I was gone before you turned to glimpse me.
Your hope I would follow you into the light—
That was only a poet's faith in the power of music.
I followed as far as the law of Hell allowed me
And then turned back to my dark home.
For us to live together, you'd have to descend
Again to the place that chills the heart of the living.
I wouldn't want you to lie awake beside me
Straining to look on the bright side,
Spinning out plan after plan full of adventure.
I wouldn't want you to wait with patience
For my reply, to assume my lengthening silence
A thoughtful prologue. The hours would grow into years
While you dreamed up a song about our ascent
Meant for the ears of friends on our arrival.
I wouldn't want to hear it dwindle and fade
As the truth gradually came into focus
And you slowly deferred to a greater power.
Who would you be then? No one I know,
Not the man who thought his music enlarged creation.
If I could speak, child of the sun,
I'd assure you I'm still your wife.
That's why I want you to stay as long as you can
Just as you are, the mistaken
Hopeful man I married.

The Lace Maker

Holding the bobbins taut as she moves the pins,
She leans in close, inches away from the fabric
Fretted and framed on the wooden work board.

A young woman in a yellow dress
Whose lighter hair, bound tight to her head
But flowing about one shoulder,

Suggests the self-forgetful beauty of service,
Service to a discipline. Just so the painting
Forgets the background to focus on her.

Here she is, so close to the surface
The painter could touch her if he stretched his hand.
Close work in sympathy with close work.

The sewing cushion holding the colored threads
Suggests a painter's palette. So Vermeer
Offers a silent tribute to another artist

Who's increasing the number of beautiful
Useless things available in a world
That would be darker and smaller without them.

This is no time to ask if the woman
Wishes she were rich enough to buy the likeness,
If Vermeer can afford the lace she's making;

No time to consider them bandying compliments.
They work in silence, and you may look on
Only if you quiet your thoughts enough

To hear the click of her needles as you lean in close
(But not so close that you cast a shadow)
And the light touch of his brush on canvas.

Progressive Health

We here at Progressive Health would like to thank you
For being one of the generous few who've promised
To bequeath your vital organs to whoever needs them.

Now we'd like to give you the opportunity
To step out far in front of the other donors
By acting a little sooner than you expected,

Tomorrow, to be precise, the day you're scheduled
To come in for your yearly physical. Six patients
Are waiting this very minute in intensive care

Who will likely die before another liver
And spleen and pairs of lungs and kidneys
Match theirs as closely as yours do. Twenty years,

Maybe more, are left you, granted, but the gain
Of these patients might total more than a century.
To you, of course, one year of your life means more

Than six of theirs, but to no one else,
No one as concerned with the general welfare
As you've claimed to be. As for your poems—

The few you may have it in you to finish—
Even if we don't judge them by those you've written,
Even if we assume you finally stage a breakthrough,

It's doubtful they'll raise one Lazarus from a grave
Metaphoric or literal. But your body is guaranteed
To work six wonders. As for the gaps you'll leave

As an aging bachelor in the life of friends,
They'll close far sooner than the open wounds
Soon to be left in the hearts of husbands and wives,

Parents and children, by the death of the six
Who now are failing. Just imagine how grateful
They'll all be when they hear of your grand gesture.

Summer and winter they'll visit your grave, in shifts,
For as long as they live, and stoop to tend it,
And leave it adorned with flowers or holly wreaths,

While your friends, who are just as forgetful
As you are, just as liable to be distracted,
Will do no more than a makeshift job of upkeep.

If the people you'll see tomorrow pacing the halls
Of our crowded facility don't move you enough,
They'll make you at least uneasy. No happy future

Is likely in store for a man like you whose conscience
Will ask him to certify every hour from now on
Six times as full as it was before, your work

Six times as strenuous, your walks in the woods
Six times as restorative as anyone else's.
Why be a drudge, staggering to the end of your life

Under this crushing burden when, with a single word,
You could be a god, one of the few gods
Who, when called on, really listens?

More Art

Why drive home to your empty house and your plans,
Still vague, for grasping life by the forelock
When across the street from the bank where your job
In home loans may soon prove expendable
The action's already begun on the big screen
Of the Granger Theater. Come watch
As a pale-faced stewardess runs down the aisle
To the row where a man sits with a notebook
Long past midnight, when everyone else is sleeping.
He's taken the flight from Spokane to Cleveland
More than a hundred times without incident;
But now as he tinkers with his five-part program
For safe investments and early retirement,
He feels a hand on his shoulder, and looking up
Faces the pale stewardess, who motions him forward,
Up to the cockpit. The pilot has had a stroke
And the drunk copilot can't be wakened.
So the man, who looks from your vantage point
High in the balcony like your brother Herman,
Straps himself in to confront, five miles above Ohio,
A yard-high panel of flashing lights
While a crackly voice comes over the radio.
It's the flight controller, Miss Wu,
Who promises to lead him step by step
To a happy landing, though her wobbling pitch
Suggests she's never before talked anyone down.
Hard for you to sit still and watch in silence,
Given your joy that a man who drove to the airport
Two hours early, fearful of heavy traffic,
Is having a real adventure thrust upon him.
Now above the static he hears the sound of rustling
As Miss Wu unfolds a drawing of the instrument screen

The better to tell him how to control his wobbling.
And then the scene shifts to her desk, the photograph
Of her young father, newly arrived from China,
Ready to scrimp and save so his baby girl
Can go to school as long as she wants to.
And then the camera lifts to the girl grown up,
Her face intent as she gives directions,
Her hair tied in a ponytail. From your seat it's clear
She looks less like the cherished daughter of Mr. Lee,
The owner of Northtown Hardware, and more like a twin
Of the girl who irons your shirts in the Granger laundry
A block from the theater. An orphan, you heard once,
When you asked the owner, for you've been curious
And now you know why. Someone should bring her here
To watch as her sister urges your brother the pilot
Not to lose hope as the houses below, small a moment ago,
Loom suddenly large. Be with him now
As he looks for a makeshift runway. Be with him
As he gropes for the switch to lower the landing gear.
This is the way to learn, right on the job,
From a teacher with a soft, musical voice
That makes you glad you're not at home by the phonograph
Trying to teach yourself to dance with a broom,
Your self-help chart of the steps taped to the floor.

Bashō

When my tastes seem too haphazard and disjointed
To compose a character, it's a comfort
To think of them as inherited from my ancestors,
Each expressing through me ancient inflections.

My need before supper to stroll to the reservoir
May indicate on my father's side nomadic origins,
The blood of a captive from Scythia who was sold
To a family in Lombardy in need of a plowman.

His marriage to a slave girl from Carthage
Explains why sea air smells so familiar,
Why I like the look of whitewashed houses on hillsides
And painted tile from Tunisia or Morocco.

To be a vehicle for the dead to speak through,
Surely that's an improvement over being a showman
Who shifts his costume to please a moody audience.
It's a comfort as long as I've many dead to choose from,

Free to trace my talent for telling stories
At a moment's notice in the style of Odysseus
All the way back on my mother's side
To a black-bearded Smyrna merchant.

His skill makes me a star at the tourist bureau
When I'm asked for ideas to make Lake Erie
More glamorous than it is in the current brochures,
The photographs more arresting, the copy spicier.

Good thing for the tourists I've also inherited
Truth-telling genes from the Hebrew prophets

That keep me from claiming our seagulls special,
As musical as the nightingale and as retiring.

So many dispositions, but no reason to worry
About caulking and splicing them into unity.
Each ancient voice asks to be kept distinct,
A separate species of tree in a crowded forest,

Cedar and pine, oak, ash, and cherry.
It isn't an accident, as I sit in the yard reading poems
Under the hemlock, that I'm drawn to Bashō.
It's clear that his blood flows in my veins,

Clear he's my father or else my twin
Misplaced at birth in a shorthanded village hospital.
How else explain that a poem of his
Is nearer to me than the proverbs of seven uncles?

Witness the first haiku in the new translation
I bought this morning at Niagara Books:
"Even in Kyoto, hearing the cuckoo's cry,
I long for Kyoto."

Improbable Story

Far from here, in the probable world,
The stable reign of the dinosaurs
Hasn't been brought to a sudden, unlooked-for end
By a billion-to-one crash with an asteroid
Ten miles across at impact, or a comet.

No dust cloud there darkens the sky
Till it snuffs out half the kingdom of vegetation,
As it might in a B movie from Hollywood,
And half the animal families,
The heavy feeders and breathers among them.

The dinosaurs rule the roost over there,
And the mammals, forced to keep hidden,
Only survive as pygmies. No time for the branching
That leads to us. None of our lean-tos or igloos,
Churches or silos, dot the landscape,

No schools or prisons. Not a single porch
Where you can sit as you're sitting here
Writing to Martha that your fog has lifted,
That despite the odds against transformation
You've left the age of ambivalence far behind you.

Over there, in the probable world, your "yes"
Means what it always has, "Who knows?"
Your "maybe" means that your doubts are overwhelming.
Martha doesn't believe one sentence as she reads
In the shade of a willow that could never survive

The winter's killer ice storms. No purple martins return
In the probable world to the little house you made them,

Ready to eat in a week their weight in mosquitoes
While Martha completes a letter that over there
She'll never be foolish enough to begin.

Bishop Berkeley

Maybe the material world would have seemed to him
Real enough, his doubts mostly illusion,
If his boyhood had been less bookish.
Maybe if he'd grown up on a farm,
A glass of milk left on his desk by a servant
To help him ease into sleep would have seemed like more
Than a prop in a play, and the wall of books behind it
Would have looked more solid than a painted backdrop.
The glass might have recalled his milking days,
The boy in the barn with Madge, the Guernsey.
Few arguments then could have convinced him
That he merely dreamed the warmth of her fur,
The ripe barn smell, the weight of the pail
As he carried it, waving the flies away, to the kitchen.
Then the Bishop might have turned his philosophy
To questions a farmer might ask on Sunday evening
Like the deepest difference between the perspective of cows
And that of the man who keeps the herd.
Is it their failure to guess the fate that awaits them
While we, intent on the truth, guess ours,
Or do they know something unknown to us
That keeps them quiet and uncomplaining,
Free of the wish for triumph or travel? Even today
A farmer might read that chapter with profit
Before he turns to wonder why his wife's awakened
Each morning for three weeks running with a dream of Prague,
The city she left with her family when she was five.
Why have those buried images shaken loose
From the bottom of the pond just now, after thirty years,
And floated up till the woman won't rest
Till she compares the city she still recalls
To the one that's bound to be disappointing?

Soon near the outskirts of Prague, in a budget motel,
The farmer will lie beside her listening to the road noise.
It's too far for him to glimpse the roof of his barn,
Which the Bishop doesn't think solid anyway,
But he can almost hear, when the traffic slows,
The sound of the cows crossing the gravel path,
And then their softer steps on the grass of the pasture,
And then their stillness as they bend to browse.

Sunrise

The Aztecs may not, after all, have been brutal,
Though they believed the sun wouldn't rise
Unless the shrines of the sun god reeked with the odor
Of human blood. Maybe their notion of debt
Was stricter than ours. What could they pay the sun
For the priceless gift of corn but men and women
With their lives before them, young and happy?

As for a god who didn't expect repayment,
Who was happy to give as long as our species
Showed it was grateful, more a parent than lender—
That notion was no more rational than the other
And far less likely to explain disaster,
Though in the long run it proved as practical
As other great inventions, the lever, the wheel.

Just the token first fruits of the field,
Just the firstlings among the calves and lambs
Sacrificed in the Temple to the sound of chanting.
And when the Romans pulled the Temple down,
The scattered worshipers decided upon a god
Who was willing to come with them into exile,
To forgo his rich diet of cattle
And make do with a bowl of peas or lentils
Left in the night at the door of a widow's cottage.

For a god so loyal, his people were willing
To overlook his inability to protect them,
Taking the blame on themselves instead.
And didn't their refusal to cast a shadow

On his reputation for justice win them an extra
Ounce of forgiveness when they tried his patience?

They tried his patience on days when the law
Felt to them like a burden, not like a blessing,
But by most evenings they'd worked their way,
Grumbling, back to acceptance. And at night,
Worn out from the effort, they slept hard,
And hours later were sleeping still
When the sun god they didn't worship
Rose in the dark on his own to feed his horses,
Just as his sunny nature prompted,
And hitch his golden chariot.

Eternal Poetry

How to grow old with grace and firmness
Is the kind of eternal problem that poetry
Is best reserved for, unaging poetry
That isn't afraid of saying what time will do
To our taste and talents, our angles of observation.
As for a local problem mentioned in passing
In this morning's news, like the cut in food stamps,
It's handled more effectively in an essay
With graphs and numbers. A poem's no proper place
To dwell on the prison reforms my friend proposes
Based on his twenty-year stint inside the walls.
In an essay there's room to go into details
So the State of New York can solve the problem
Once and for all and turn to issues more lasting.
Facing old age, the theme I'm developing here,
Will still be an issue when the failure of prisons
Interests only historians of our backward era.
A poem's the place to answer the question
Whether it's best to disdain old age as a pest
Or respect it as a mighty army or welcome it
As a guest with a ton of baggage. Three options
That health-care professionals might deem too harsh
To appear in their journals. I wish they would help
My friend publish his essay on prison reform,
His practical plan to inspire the inmates
By cutting their minimum sentences if they master a trade
So they won't return, as is likely now, in a year or two.
The odds are long against getting the ear of the governor
But not impossible if he's only a year from retirement
And old age prompts him to earn a paragraph
In the history of reform. The bill might squeak through
If the Assembly decides it hasn't the wherewithal

To keep old prisons in decent repair
Let alone build new ones. No money now
To pay the prison inspector what he deserves
As he makes his rounds in his battered pickup.
An old man shaking his head in disgust
At the roof leaks, peeling plaster, and rusty plumbing
That might have been avoided with a little foresight
And therefore don't deserve a place in a poem.
And to think he's been at it for thirty years
Despite his vow, after a month on the job,
To be out of it at the latest by Christmas.
Nobody's eager to wear his shoes
Unless we count the people inside the walls
Whose envy of those growing old outside
Is a constant always to be relied on,
And so can enter a poem at any time.

In the Short Term

There's no denying that the only joy
Likely to last lies in our power completely,
As the Stoics say, not in the power of others.

The joy, for example, of placing one's life in harmony
With laws that reason deduces to be eternal,
Of doing our work as it should be done—
No cutting corners to speed delivery,
No rushing to finish the job before closing time.
No closing time in fact, so long as the work is pleasing.

The joy of winning glory among one's fellows,
However sweet, lasts only until the fellows
Sail off for better jobs overseas.
Lucky for them if they learn to become
The citizens of the world that the Stoics say
We should all become, indifferent to local applause
From Romans, Egyptians, Medes, or Athenians.

There's no denying fame-hungry Alcibiades
Thrusts up on sand a magnificent tower
That threatens his neighbors' roofs as well as his own.
Shame on him for wrecking the peace talks with Sparta
So he could have the war he longed to shine in
And be cheered the loudest when he strolled the agora.

An hour after his fleet set sail for Sicily, his enemies,
In envy of all the glory soon to be his, were working
To turn the minds of the crowd against him.
Too bad he didn't agree with Socrates
On the nourishment that the rational soul requires,

Different from praise, to become immortal,
The praise that Homer was wrong to bestow on war.

There's no denying insight to Epictetus
When he argues the story of Troy is about illusion,
That Paris was crazy to endanger his town for the sheen
Of a woman's body, Helen crazy to love a playboy,
Menelaus to think a wife as wayward as his
Worth regaining. As for Achilles, whatever possessed him
To squabble with Agamemnon over a war prize?

All dust now, Troy as much as the flesh of Helen,
Though Homer never assumes they're immortal,
Just that you won't be likely to forget them quickly
Once their story is told in the leisurely way
It should be told, over many evenings.

Time enough to make clear that fault-ridden Paris
Is loved by a goddess, that Helen's a gift
Only a goddess could have provided.
And who is he to deny a goddess
Even if her gift only lasts a day?

Guardian Angel

Not the angel that helps you resist temptation
(Conscience and heart are enough for that,
And, besides, when have you been tempted lately?),
But the one with advice about tactics
For possessing your share of the true and beautiful.
The one who tells you the plaid of your jacket
Will prove too loud for the soft-spoken sensitive woman
You're destined to meet tonight in line at the theater
When everything depends on a first impression.

With the angel's help you can open a conversation
On a fruitful subject like happiness and explain
People are wrong to seek it directly,
How it comes on the back of other things
Like losing oneself in a casual conversation
That tests our powers of empathy, not cleverness.

A practical angel, ignorant in philosophy
But peerless in group dynamics, who can show you
Why it's unwise to urge your hesitant friend
To leave her apartment for yours too quickly,
How a sudden fear of confinement may choke off feelings
That otherwise would be sure to bloom.

And if eagerness wins out over prudence, the angel,
Instead of saying, "I told you so," will help you
Turn from errors that can't be altered
And sally out in quest of a local problem
Where your many talents can make a difference.

Why not get involved with the block-club committee
Dedicated to stopping the corner drugstore

From tripling in size and knocking down in the process
Houses that keep the scale of the neighborhood human?
Soon you may find yourself toasting the cause
By candlelight with your eager co-chair,
A woman fearless in the face of officialdom.

It's true if she had an angel to help her
She wouldn't be wearing the dress she's wearing,
A duplicate of the one your mother wore
Thirty summers ago at Cape May when your father
Embarked full-time on his career of drinking.
But doesn't this ignorance, which her angel
Should have dispelled, make her appealing
To someone like you, who's quick to discern a soul mate?

As you sit across the table you can feel your heart
Swell with so much sympathy that your jacket
Feels tight in the chest, your loud plaid jacket.
"Why not remove it," the angel you need would ask,
"And drape it out of sight on the back of your chair?"

May Jen

This is the evening I was hoping for,
The one when my bad times are transposed to stories
Offered as a small return for the story you've just told me
Here at this window table in the May Jen restaurant
On rain-washed Elmwood. How once,
When drink had driven your dad from the family,
Meeting you on the street, he gave you his promise,
In a voice cold sober, to send you the dress
You needed for confirmation, and how you felt
When it never arrived. A sad story
That makes me happy I've carried for years
Memories that till this evening I've never valued.

This is the rainy April evening toward which our lives,
Despite the odds, have been moving for decades
Along different paths, without our knowing,
So we might notice through this rain-streaked window
How the glinting streetlamps and street reflections,
Stoplights and traffic, set off by contrast
Our easy calm, our stillness.

This is the conversation that can have no midpoint,
However clear its beginning, if it has no end.
And why would we turn to ask for the bill,
Why don our raincoats and walk to the car
And join the pitiful traffic that has to make do
With the dream of a life behind it or a life ahead?
The past we need is only a kind of currency
Stamped in red with the date of this day.
And the fabulous future is beginning to understand
If it wants to meet us it will have to swallow its pride
And come to our table, not wait for us to come looking,
For we have no plans to go anywhere.

Eternal Life

An immortal soul, that's something for me to wish for,
To be off on a long trek after my body's buried
And my friends have driven away from the graveyard.

Where am I headed? Not downward, if I'm permitted
To judge by the rules of fairness as I conceive them,
For nothing I've done seems ripe for eternal punishment.

Not upward, for nothing seems worthy of eternal bliss.
Odds are I'll stay where I am, forever earthbound,
And face the problem of filling the endless return

Of earthly summers and autumns, winters and springs.
It won't be easy for a being retired from action,
A shadow too weak even to hold open a door

When a friend among the living, bearing a tea tray,
Steps out to join her guests on the verandah.
The conversation should hold my interest all evening

Even if I can't participate, my voice too small.
But later, when strangers fill the familiar rooms,
I'll seem to be listening to a script that's conventional,

To acting forced and wooden, and slip outside.
What then? Do I keep my distance from other ghosts
Or join them in sharing stories about the old days

In cricket whispers? Either way, I'll wonder about the joy
I imagined coming my way with death behind me,
Not looming ahead, and leisure, so scarce before,

Suddenly limitless. Not much solace is likely
When I compare the vague ghosts of my friends
With the living originals, whose particular lusters

Can't be divorced from their lifelong gloom on birthdays,
Their protests against their mirrors, their witty admissions
In listing the enemies that creased their foreheads

And slowed their pace to a hobble, and made them forgetful,
Though they remembered their promises well enough
And tried to keep many till death released them.

But how can ghosts swear loyalty to the end
If there is no end for them, only a boundless ocean;
Or does a truth I haven't a map to now

Wait in my ghostly existence to be discovered? If not,
It won't surprise me if I find myself on my knees
Cupping my hands with others at the river's edge

To sip forgetfulness. No surprise if I'm ferried back,
Oblivious, to be born again in the flesh
Among strangers it will take me years to recognize.

The God Who Loves You

It must be troubling for the god who loves you
To ponder how much happier you'd be today
Had you been able to glimpse your many futures.
It must be painful for him to watch you on Friday evenings
Driving home from the office, content with your week—
Three fine houses sold to deserving families—
Knowing as he does exactly what would have happened
Had you gone to your second choice for college,
Knowing the roommate you'd have been allotted
Whose ardent opinions on painting and music
Would have kindled in you a lifelong passion.
A life thirty points above the life you're living
On any scale of satisfaction. And every point
A thorn in the side of the god who loves you.
You don't want that, a large-souled man like you
Who tries to withhold from your wife the day's disappointments
So she can save her empathy for the children.
And would you want this god to compare your wife
With the woman you were destined to meet on the other campus?
It hurts you to think of him ranking the conversation
You'd have enjoyed over there higher in insight
Than the conversation you're used to.
And think how this loving god would feel
Knowing that the man next in line for your wife
Would have pleased her more than you ever will
Even on your best days, when you really try.
Can you sleep at night believing a god like that
Is pacing his cloudy bedroom, harassed by alternatives
You're spared by ignorance? The difference between what is
And what could have been will remain alive for him
Even after you cease existing, after you catch a chill
Running out in the snow for the morning paper,

Losing eleven years that the god who loves you
Will feel compelled to imagine scene by scene
Unless you come to the rescue by imagining him
No wiser than you are, no god at all, only a friend
No closer than the actual friend you made at college,
The one you haven't written in months. Sit down tonight
And write him about the life you can talk about
With a claim to authority, the life you've witnessed,
Which for all you know is the life you've chosen.

CARL DENNIS is the author of eight other books of poetry, including, most recently, *Practical Gods,* which in 2002 was awarded the Pulitzer Prize in poetry. In 2000 he received the Ruth Lilly Prize from *Poetry Magazine* and the Modern Poetry Association for his contribution to American poetry. He lives in Buffalo, where he is Artist in Residence at the State University of New York, and is a sometime member of the faculty of the MFA Program in creative writing at Warren Wilson College.

PENGUIN POETS

Ted Berrigan
Selected Poems
The Sonnets

Philip Booth
Lifelines

Jim Carroll
Fear of Dreaming
Void of Course

Carl Dennis
New and Selected Poems
1974–2004
Practical Gods

Barbara Cully
Desire Reclining

Diane di Prima
Loba

Stuart Dischell
Dig Safe

Stephen Dobyns
Pallbearers Envying the
One Who Rides
The Porcupine's Kisses

Roger Fanning
Homesick

Amy Gerstler
Crown of Weeds
Ghost Girl
Medicine
Nerve Storm

Debora Greger
Desert Fathers, Uranium
Daughters
God

Robert Hunter
Sentinel

Barbara Jordan
Trace Elements

Mary Karr
Viper Rum

Jack Kerouac
Book of Blues
Book of Haikus

Joanne Kyger
As Ever

Ann Lauterbach
If in Time
On a Stair

Phyllis Levin
Mercury

William Logan
Macbeth in Venice
Night Battle
Vain Empires

Derek Mahon
Selected Poems

Michael McClure
Huge Dreams:
San Francisco and
Beat Poems

Carol Muske
An Octave Above
Thunder

Alice Notley
The Descent of Alette
Disobedience
Mysteries of Small Houses

Lawrence Raab
The Probable World
Visible Signs

Stephanie Strickland
V

Anne Waldman
Kill or Cure
Marriage: A Sentence

Philip Whalen
Overtime: Selected
Poems

Robert Wrigley
Lives of the Animals
Reign of Snakes

John Yau
Borrowed Love Poems